THE DEVIL'S I

A History of the Written Word in Western Magic from Ancient Egypt to the Present Day.

Front cover illustration:
'Witches Sabbath' by Frans Francken (1581-1642)
(The Bridgeman Art Library).

THE DEVIL'S BOOKSHELF

A History of the Written Word in Western Magic from Ancient Egypt to the Present Day

CHRISTOPHER McINTOSH

THE AQUARIAN PRESS
Wellingborough, Northamptonshire

First published 1985

British Library Cataloguing in Publication Data

McIntosh, Christopher
The Devil's Bookshelf : a history of grimoires and books of spells.
1. Magic—History
I. Title
133.4'3'09 BF1589

ISBN 0-85030-247-1

The Aquarian Press is part of the Thorsons Publishing Group

Printed and bound in Great Britain

The world of Magian mankind is filled with a fairy-tale feeling. Devils and evil spirits threaten man; angels and fairies protect him. There are talismans, mysterious lands, cities, buildings, and beings, secret letters, Solomon's Seal, the Philosophers' Stone. And over all this is poured the quivering cavern-light that the spectral darkness ever threatens to swallow up.

Oswald Spengler, *The Decline of the West,* Volume II, Chapter 8.

To my sons
Angus and Jason
with love

CONTENTS

ACKNOWLEDGEMENTS

I wish to express my particular thanks to the following people: Michael Cox, whose idea it was that I should write this book; R.A. Gilbert for generous advice, helpful criticism and the loan of material; Lionel Snell for his first-hand account of the Abra-Melin working; Hilmar Hilmarsson for reading the manuscript and making useful comments; Gisela Kirberg for encouragement and for typing a large part of the book; also Paul Baines, John Hamill, Zachary Cox, Adam McLean, Stephen Skinner, Marian Green, and Kathleen and Geraldine Collins of the Atlantis Bookshop. I must also thank the publishers of material quoted in the text, whose names are recorded in the chapter notes.

INTRODUCTION

This book is about the role played in magic by the written word. It is not, despite its title, essentially about 'black magic', a term which in any case serves little purpose except to provide journalists of the popular press with material for such headlines as 'BLACK MAGIC SEX RITES OF THE CLAPHAM WITCHES'. At the same time it must be recognized that there are debased as well as higher forms of magic, and both are dealt with here in so far as they are reflected in written or printed material. Indeed, the debasement and corruption of magical traditions in text and therefore in practice is an important part of this story, and in many ways a fascinating one.

My own contact with the world of magic began when, as an undergraduate at Oxford, I became simultaneously interested in astrology and in the works of Aleister Crowley, perhaps the most famous magician of recent times. In a deliciously stygian basement bookshop in my home town of Edinburgh I bought a copy of Crowley's *Magick in Theory and Practice,* a four-volume work in an orange paper binding with a curious six-pointed star on the cover. This was the first 'grimoire' (using the term in its wider sense) that I ever acquired.

Many years later I had the good fortune to meet a man who had been Crowley's chief disciple for a number of years and who possessed the largest collection of Crowleyana in the world. He had joined Crowley's group, the Astrum Argentinum, in 1927 and had taken the magical name of *Volo Intelligere* ('I wish to understand').

One summer day in 1969 I went to see Brother Volo Intelligere at his house in Gloucestershire, taking with me a friend who shared my interest in Crowley. Our host received us warmly and during the course of the day talked to us at length about Crowley. Sitting in his beautiful garden, we were shown a fascinating collection of mementoes, including a talisman which Brother Volo Intelligere had used for finding books for his Crowley collection. It was a small piece of paper about two inches square, covered with Qabalistic sigils in black ink and bearing some curious stains which it appeared were the remains of the semen and menstrual blood which had been used to consecrate it. This, we were told, was originally the talisman that Crowley had used when he wanted to find a new Scarlet Woman (the term he used for his magical and sexual companion). I had the sense that I was looking at something possessing an archaic energy of great potency.

From a twentieth-century garden in Gloucestershire to the Egypt of the Pharoahs is a long way in both time and space, but that talisman was a direct link between the two, for it represented a magical tradition stretching back to ancient Egypt and beyond.

This is an example of how magic has survived through the centuries, handed down partly by word of mouth and partly through written texts. While the oral tradition is important, magic would not have survived in its present form had it not been enshrined in books and manuscripts. Clearly, therefore, some knowledge of the history of these texts is important for an understanding of the western magical tradition.

Works of practical magic are often referred to as grimoires (a corruption of the French word *grammaire,* meaning grammar) or clavicles (from the Latin *clavicula,* meaning key). In the narrow sense these are books of practical instruction to which you turn if you have a specific aim which you wish to attain by magical means. If we compare magical forces to electricity, then grimoires are books of electrical instruction. They tell you about different types of current and circuit and how to avoid the danger of electrocution. But in fact it is impossible to separate the purely practical side of grimoires from the religious and philosophical *Weltanschauung* to which they belong.

Magic grows out of religion, and the grimoires belong to

a religious tradition. They have their antecedents in the ancient ritual texts of Egypt and Persia. With the coming of Christianity the old religions were gradually suppressed. Their gods were banished, their altars trampled on, their books destroyed. But the magical practices belonging to these religions lived on — like a body whose head has been amputated but which stubbornly refuses to lie down. This is what we are looking at when we look at the grimoires. They are remnants of a great tradition. Some of them remain faithful to the spirit of that tradition, others reflect a debasement of it. Seen in this light, the grimoires take on a new significance. They are — to borrow G.R.S. Mead's phrase in the title of his book on the Gnosis — 'fragments of a faith forgotten'.

Part I

Magical Writings Through the Ages

1.
THE WORLD OF THE MAGICIAN

In order to enter into a study of magical writings it is first of all necessary to understand what is meant by the term 'magic'. James Hastings, in his *Encyclopaedia of Religion and Ethics,* states that 'in any general treatment of the subject of magic the problem of its definition must occupy the chief place, seeing that it constitutes a veritable storm-centre in the anthropological literature of the present day.' He continues: 'The word is descended from the Greek *mageia* (μαγεια) and Latin *magia* which, strictly speaking, refer to the religion, learning and occult practices of the Persian Magi or priests of Zoroaster, in the form in which these became known in the West.' [1] This Persian system, being widely misunderstood, was regarded with suspicion in Europe. Hence the word 'magic' tended from the start to carry an unfavourable connotation, implying something both superstitious and sinister. Thus later on, when anthropologists began to study the beliefs and practices of so-called 'primitive' peoples, they used the word 'magic' to describe the activities of the witch doctor, the shaman, the rain maker and the Voodoo priest.

Typical of the anthropologist's view of magic is that expressed by Sir James Frazer in *The Golden Bough.* Frazer declares that 'magic is a spurious system of natural law as well as a fallacious guide of conduct; it is a false science as well as an abortive art'. At the same time he sees magic as 'next of kin to science' since the two have in common the 'general assumption of a succession of events determined by law'. Nevertheless magic as he sees it is only the 'bastard sister of science'. He goes on to say that 'all magic is necessarily false and barren; for were it ever to become true and fruitful it would no longer be magic but science.'[2]

It is also significant that the word has come to be used, in a different but related sense, to describe the activities of the stage conjuror. Here the term signifies the bringing about of apparently miraculous effects through the clever use of illusion. Interestingly, today's man in the street will tend to think of 'magic' as being what the conjuror does and to look upon anything else as 'black magic'.

So the practice of magic is popularly seen as involving one or more of the following: (a) a wish to strive after miraculous effects, illusory or otherwise; (b) a superstitious and primitive mentality; (c) an intention to deceive; (d) an attempt to apply incorrectly interpreted laws and connections; (e) an unhealthy wish to manipulate the powers of evil.

At the same time there have been, through the ages, individuals who have attempted to cling more closely to the original meaning of magic and to defend it against those who have misunderstood and criticized it. Roger Bacon, for example, in the thirteenth century tried to rehabilitate magic as a form of operative science. Furthermore, many of the grimoires and Rosicrucian texts of the seventeenth and eighteenth centuries begin by outlining the pedigree of an ancient wisdom which they often refer to as 'magic' or 'magia' and which they trace back either to Zoroaster or to the ancient Egyptians. It is this concept of magic that has been resurrected in recent times by the modern school of 'ritual' magicians, stemming largely from the Hermetic Order of the Golden Dawn, which will be discussed in a later chapter. The twentieth-century magician, Aleister Crowley, who spelt the word with a 'k', gave the following definition. 'Magick is the science and art of causing change to occur in conformity with will.'[3] Two more recent writers on the subject, Francis King and Stephen Skinner, in their *Techniques of High Magic*, give a similar definition: magic is 'the art and science of using little known natural forces in order to achieve changes in consciousness and the physical environment.' They add that they use the word also 'in a secondary sense as meaning the entire body of doctrines and techniques concerning the conjuration, nature and power of angels, spirits, demons and other non-human entities' as well as the making and consecration of magical weapons and talismans, ritual divination and the exploration of universes other than the one familiar to us. [4]

The essential ingredients in the kind of magic described by Crowley, King and Skinner are will and imagination. The imagination is inflamed by the use of certain potent images, symbols, sensory experiences and ritual formulae and is then placed at the service of the will to bring about whatever changes are desired. These changes may be within the magician himself or within the material world, or both. They can also obviously be for good or evil.

We tend to find similar assumptions behind the magic of all ages and cultures. The first is that everything in the universe is linked by a network of correspondences. To give an example, a modern magician who works with the Golden Dawn system considers that the planet Mercury, fish, the colour orange and the number eight are all connected. Thus an invocation of Mercury might be preceded by the consuming of fish and the sounding of eight knocks. The same sort of correspondences can be found in the magical systems of African witch doctors, North American shamans and Aborigine medicine men.

Related to this notion is the idea that man is a microcosm of the universe. This underlies, for example, the astrological view that each sign of the zodiac corresponds to a part of the body and that each planet is echoed by a force or drive in the human character.

Another assumption found in magic is that all things are governed by conscious entities whose behaviour can, to some extent, be influenced by the magician. Gods can be placated by sacrifice or prayer. Demons can be constrained and commanded through the use of appropriate ritual based on the system of correspondences. Although the magician may not always have a deity or supernatural entity in mind when he works a spell there is usually an implicit belief in the existence of such entities.

Thus magic is very close to religion, and it is difficult to make a hard and fast distinction between magical ceremony and a religious one. Broadly one could say that in the former the magician is in the posture of a controlling technician, whereas in the latter the priest is in a posture of supplication to the divine powers. Nevertheless there are religious rituals that are magical in nature and magical rituals that are distinctly religious.

By now the reader should have an idea of the diversity of meaning contained in the word 'magic'. In this book I shall not be discussing stage conjuring nor the practices of African rain makers, and I shall touch only incidentally on so-called 'black' magic. I shall concentrate on the body of magical tradition that is known to us in the western world, excluding alchemy which I shall only touch on briefly as it would demand a separate study. I shall also include a certain amount of information about oriental, chiefly Tibetan, magic on account of its striking parallels with the western form.

2
The Roots of the Occult Tradition

The characteristics of the magical universe as we know it — its geography, its hierarchy of gods, angels and demons — were drawn from a number of ancient sources. It was the Babylonians, for example, who first developed the rudiments of western astrology, a very important part of the magical tradition. They discovered the distinction between the stars and planets and established the traditional astrological system of seven moving heavenly bodies: Sun, Moon, Mercury, Venus, Mars, Jupiter and Saturn. These correspond to seven Babylonian deities. Venus, for example, was linked with the goddess Ishtar. The Babylonians also established the basic characteristics that are still associated with the planets today: Mercury with cleverness, Mars with aggression, Venus with love, and so on.

But Babylonia was only one of the civilizations that contributed to the development of western magic. Even more important in this respect were the ancient Egyptians. In fact magic as it is known today would not exist but for Egypt. One of the most informative writers on this subject is E.A. Wallis Budge, whose *Egyptian Magic* is worth quoting from at some length.[1] Budge writes in his preface:

> A study of the remains of the native religious literature of ancient Egypt which have come down to us has revealed the fact that the belief in magic, that is to say, in the power of magical names, and spells, and enchantments, and formulae, and pictures and figures, and amulets, and in the performance of ceremonies accompanied by the utterance of words of power, to produce supernatural results, formed a large and important part of Egyptian religion … this belief

> influenced their minds and, from the earliest to the latest period of their history, shaped their views concerning things temporal as well as spiritual ...
>
> Egyptian magic dates from the time when the pre-dynastic and prehistoric dwellers in Egypt believed that the earth, and the underworld, and the air, and the sky were peopled with countless beings, visible and invisible, which were held to be friendly or unfriendly to man according as the operations of nature, which they were supposed to direct, were favourable or unfavourable to him ... the chief object of magic was to give man pre-eminence over such beings.
>
> The magic of most early nations aimed at causing the transference of power from a supernatural being to man ... but the object of Egyptian magic was to endow man with the means of compelling both friendly and hostile powers, nay, at a later time, even God Himself, to do what he wished, whether they were willing or not.

The power of the ancient Egyptian priest, says Budge, was considered to be almost boundless. He only had to pronounce certain words in the proper tone of voice and accompanied by the right ceremonial formulae and he was enabled to cast out evil spirits, cure sickness and control the wind and rain. Budge goes on to make an important observation:

> Now if views such as these concerning the magician's power were held by the educated folk of ancient Egypt there is little to wonder at when we find that beliefs and superstitions of the most degraded character flourished with rank luxuriance among the peasants and working classes of that country, who failed to understand the symbolism of the elaborate ceremonies which were performed in the temples, and who were too ignorant to distinguish the spiritual conceptions which lay at their root. To meet the religious needs of such people the magician, and in later times the priest, found it necessary to provide pageants and ceremonies which appealed chiefly to the senses, and following their example, unscrupulous but clever men took advantage of the ignorance of the general public and pretended to knowledge of the supernatural and laid claim to the possession of power over gods, and spirits, and demons. Such false knowledge and power they sold for money, and for purposes of gain the so-called magician was ready to further any sordid

> transaction or wicked scheme which his dupe wished to carry out. This magic degenerated into sorcery, and demonology, and witchcraft, and those who dealt in it were regarded as associates of the Devil, and servants of the powers of darkness, and workers of the 'black art'. In the 'white' and 'black' magic of the Egyptians most of the magic known in the other countries of the world may be found ...

All this is extremely interesting because it shows that as early as ancient Egyptian times a distinction had opened up between a higher and a lower type of magic. This is a distinction which we shall see perpetuated all through the history of magical literature. In fact there are today countless echoes of the world of Egyptian occultism. If the Pharoah Akhenaten were to be reincarnated in modern London he would not need to go to the Egyptian gallery at the Britsh museum in order to feel at home; hanging from the necks of young passers-by or displayed on the stalls of street traders he would see familiar objects such as the ankh and the eye of Horus, symbols from the venerable *Book of the Dead*, the collection of complex funerary rites designed to ensure the safe passage of the soul to paradise. This and other Egyptian religious books were written out by priestly scribes who were employed in large numbers to provide copies of the sacred texts.

Then, as now, the divine symbols were used for both exalted and lowly purposes. They not only formed part of the solemn funerary rites but were also worn by the common people as talismans. And then, as now, the eye of Horus, or *utchat*, was one of the commonest. It was made of gold, silver, granite, wood or various precious stones such as lapis lazuli. It was a solar talisman which enabled the deceased to become a god or, when used by the living, conferred strength and health. There were, however, two kinds of *utchat*: one facing to the right, which was light in its nature; and another, facing to the left, which was dark. The Egyptians knew very well that magic has its black as well as its white side.

Budge describes an interesting example of the use of the *utchat* which occurs in a Greek spell for the discovery of a thief, written as late as the fourth century AD. The instructions are as follows:

> Take the herb *khelbei* and *bugloss*, press out the juice and burn the crushed leaves and mix the ashes with the juice. Anoint and write upon a wall Khōo with these materials. And take a common piece of wood and cut a hammer out of it, and strike with it upon the ear, pronouncing this spell: 'I adjure thee by the holy names, render up the thief who has carried away such [and such] a thing Khalkhak, Khalkoum, Khiam, Khar, Khroum, Zbar, Bēri, Zbarkom, Khrē, Kariōb, Pharibou, and by the terrible names αεεηηηιιιιοοοοουυυυυυωωωωωωω'.

The last part of the formula quoted consists of the seven vowels of the Greek alphabet which, in the Gnostic system, were supposed to contain all the names of God. This was considered a very powerful instrument when used in a spell.

This is an example of how Egyptian magic influenced other civilizations of the ancient world. The Greeks and Romans had great respect for it, and many of them regarded Egypt as the fountainhead of occult knowledge. They took over, for example, the Egyptian system in which different symbols applied to different parts of the body and could be used for curative purposes. Another thing they borrowed from the Egyptians was the importance attached to names. It was believed that if one knew the name of a god or devil one thereby had power over him.

The ancient Egyptians also bestowed on magical books the special importance and mystique that is the subject of this study. This is clearly illustrated by the following account given by Budge of a conspiracy involving magical writings, which occurred in about 1200 BC during the reign of Rameses III.

> It seems that a number of high officials, the overseer of the Treasury included, and certain scribes, conspired together against this king, apparently with a view to dethroning him. They took into their counsels a number of ladies attached to the court ... and the chief abode of these ladies became the headquarters of the conspirators ... The conspiracy soon extended from Egypt to Ethiopia, and a military official of high rank in that country was drawn into it by his sister, who urged him to 'Incite the men to commit crime, and do thyself come to do wrong to thy lord'; now the sister of this official was in the Per-khent, and so she was able to give her brother

> the latest information of the progress of the disaffection. Not content with endeavouring to dethrone the king by an uprising of both soldiers and civilians, Hui, a certain high official, who was the overseer of the [royal] cattle, bethought him of applying magic to help their evil designs, and with this object in view he went to someone who had access to the king's library, and he obtained from him a book containing formulae of a magical nature, and directions for working magic. By means of this book he obtained 'divine power', and he became able to cast spells upon folk. Having gained possession of the book he next looked out for some place where he could carry out his magical work without interruption, and at length found one. Here he set to work to make figures of men in wax, and amulets inscribed with words of magical power which would provoke love, and these he succeeded in introducing into the royal palace by means of the official Athirmā; and it seems as if those who received them were under the magical influence of Hui. It is probable that the love philtres were intended for the use of the ladies who were involved in the conspiracy, but as to the object of the wax figures there is no doubt, for they were intended to work harm to the king. Meanwhile Hui studied his magical book with diligence, and he succeeded in finding efficacious means for carrying out all the 'horrible things and all the wickednesses which his heart could imagine'; ... In another place Hui is accused of writing books or formulae of magical words, the effect of which would be to drive men out of their senses, and to strike terror into them; ... But their efforts were in vain, the conspiracy was discovered, and the whole matter was carefully investigated by two small courts of enquiry ... Hui ... was compelled to commit suicide.

Budge concludes:

> The above story of the famous conspiracy against Rameses III is most useful as proving that books of magic existed in the Royal Library, and that they were not mere treatises on magical practices, but definite works with detailed instructions to the reader how to perform ceremonies which were necessary to make the formulae or words of power efficacious.

When the Greeks and later the Romans wanted to acquire magical knowledge it was Egypt that provided them with one of the richest sources of material. After Egypt came under Greek rule in the fourth century BC, following the conquests of Alexander the Great, the country enjoyed a marvellous fusion of Greek and Egyptian thought and religion. Ptolemy I, who was the first of the Greek kings of Egypt, made Alexandria his capital and established a great museum and library there. He also founded the cult of Serapis, based on the Greek god Pluto and the Egyptian Oserapis, a combination of Osiris and the sacred bull Apis. Under Ptolemy and his successors Graeco-Egyptian magic flourished, especially in Alexandria, and spread out from Egypt all over the Mediterranean. Right up to the early Christian era Egypt remained a great melting pot of religious and magical beliefs.

Apart from Egypt and Babylonia, the other great well-head of the magical tradition was Persia. Like Egypt, Persia came under the sway of Greece and later of Rome, with intervals when the Persian empire flourished. The ebb and flow of Persian influence left behind elements of religious and magical practice which ultimately had as great an influence on the Roman world as the worship of Isis and Osiris. The Roman emperors, in fact, went as far as to imitate the Persian concept of monarchy. Franz Cumont writes in his book *The Oriental Religions in Roman Paganism* [2]: 'The custom of carrying the sacred fire before the Caesars as an emblem of the perpetuity of their power, dated back to Darius and with other Persian traditions passed on to the dynasties that divided the empire of Alexander.' It is not surprising to learn that the emperor Commodus was initiated into the Mithras cult, which was of Persian origin, and that in the year 307 Diocletian met with Galerius and Licinus at Carnuntum on the Danube and dedicated a sanctuary there to Mithras as the protector of their empire.

The Jews provided another channel for the dissemination of Persian beliefs. Persian angelology and demonology had a great effect on Jewish popular belief and spread with it during the Jewish dispersion.

The richness of the Persian traditions can be judged from the fact that the list of works catalogued under the name of the Persian prophet Zoroaster in the great library of Alexandria contained some two million lines. 'This immense body of sacred literature', writes Cumont, 'was bound to attract the attention of scholars and to call forth the reflections of philosophers. The dim and dubious science that reached even the lower classes under the name of ''magic'' was to a considerable extent of Persian origin, as its name indicates.' Cumont refers here to the fact that the word 'mage' or 'magus' is derived from the Persian word for a sorcerer-priest.

In Asia Minor there was a strong Persian presence, and from there it was only a short step to Rome itself and thence to the Roman empire. Along with the Persian nobility in Asia Minor a clergy had also established itself. These magi, known also as *magousaioi* or *pyrethes* (fire-eaters), were present not only in Asia Minor but all over the Levant.

What was the system of belief that these magi followed? Cumont describes it as being a result of the mingling of Chaldean beliefs with the older Persian religion of Mazdaism.

> The divinities of the two religions became identified, their legends connected, and the Semitic astrology ... superimposed itself on the naturalistic myths of the Persians. Ahura Mazda was assimilated to Bel, Anahita to Ishtar, and Mithra to Shamash, the solar god. For that reason Mithra was commonly called *Sol Invictus* in the Roman mysteries, and an abstruse and complicated astronomic symbolism was always part of the teachings revealed to candidates for intitiation and manifested itself also in the artistic embellishments of the temple.

The essence of Persian religion was a dualistic system which deified the evil principle in the person of Ahriman, master of the infernal spirits, and established him as a rival to the supreme deity, Ahura Mazda, possessing equal claim to worship. This dualism began to be described by Greek and Roman writers of about the first century AD, notably Plutarch, and 'from that time', states Cumont, 'dates the appearance in literature of the anti-gods, under the command of the powers of darkness and arrayed against the celestial spirits, messengers or 'angels' of divinity. They were Ahriman's *devas* struggling with the Yazatas of Ormuzd'.

Cumont points out that the third-century writer Porphyry, in his *De Abstinentia;*

> ... shows that the earliest neo-Platonists had already admitted Persian demonology into their system. Below the incorporeal and indivisible supreme being ... there were countless spirits. Some of them, the gods of cities and nations, received special names: the others comprised a nameless multitude. They were divided into two groups. The first were the benevolent spirits ... they acted as intermediaries between gods and men ... The others were wicked spirits inhabiting regions close to the earth and there was no evil that they did not exert every effort to cause.

The worship of two deities, a light and a dark one, persisted down through the centuries and was found among the Yezidis, or devil-worshippers, of Mesopotamia. This much misunderstood sect did not worship evil but paid homage to the devil in an attempt to placate him and thus avert misfortune. Sir Austen Henry Layard, the archaeologist, in his books on Nineveh and Babylon, gives a fascinating account of a visit to a Yezidi stronghold and emphasizes the warmth and high moral character of the people.[3]

The Persian dual-deity concept also influenced Gnosticism, one of the most important systems of belief to emerge from the late Hellenic world. In the Gnostic view the world was created by the evil deity in order to trap the spirit of man, which belongs to the realm of the god of light. Man, according to the Gnostic, is imprisoned in the cavern, but there are those who possess knowledge (*gnosis*) that enables them to drill through the roof of the cavern, and this knowledge can be communicated to others. The cavern is either something to be escaped from or something to be overcome and mastered. In either case the Gnostic can be helped by appropriate rituals and magical formulae.

Another important element in the western magical tradition — perhaps the most important of all — is the culture of Judaism and particularly the hidden traditions within it, which today are grouped together under the name of Qabalah. It might appear paradoxical that a monotheistic religion such as Judaism should form a partnership with the polytheistic religions of Egypt, Babylon and Persia. But we must remember two things. First, the Jews were not always monotheistic. Before Jehovah monopolized their religion they worshipped other deities, such as the goddess Astaroth (a version of the Babylonian Ishtar or Astarte), who had a temple on Mount Sion. Her cult is believed to have survived secretly long after the Jews became officially monotheistic. The second thing that must be remembered is that the Qabalah postulates a hierarchy of forces and entities which can quite easily, in the popular mind, be married to a polytheistic system. It would be helpful here to define the Qabalah and explain some of its basic ideas.

The Qabalah is a Jewish mystical or esoteric tradition of considerable but indeterminate age. The name is derived from the Hebrew word קבל (QBL) meaning 'to receive' and hence denotes a doctrine that has been received or handed down. It is cognate with the English word cabal, meaning a secret intrigue or clique. Qabalism was studied and practised, *inter alia,* among the Jews of Islamic Spain, in sixteenth-century Palestine and among the Hasidic communities in Poland and Russia during the eighteenth and nineteenth centuries. It combines several functions, being, among other things, an attempt to illuminate the nature of God, a doctrine explaining the nature of the universe and its creation, a way of helping man to understand his place in creation and his true destiny, and a set of practical mystical and esoteric techniques.

Originally the tradition was purely an oral one, but later it became enshrined in certain texts, the best known being the *Sepher Yetsirah* (Book of Formation), a short anonymous text dating from between the third and sixth centuries AD, and the *Sepher Ha-Zohar* (Book of Splendour), dating from the thirteenth century and written down by the Spanish rabbi Moses de Leon. The first printed edition of the *Sepher Yetsirah* was the Latin version of Guillaume Postel, issued at Paris in 1552. The *Zohar* was first published at Mantua in 1558 in a Hebrew edition. Although neither of these texts is strictly speaking magical, both had a considerable influence on Qabalistic magic, as practised by both Jews and non-Jews.

The Qabalists claimed that their tradition was recorded in the Old Testament, where it lay concealed by complicated codes and ciphers. They used three methods for decoding the Bible, known as gematria, notarikon and temura. Gematria was based on the fact that each letter of the Hebrew alphabet stands for a number. Thus a word in the biblical text could be taken to stand for another word with the same numerical value. For example, the word *achad* (unity) has the same value as *aheba* (love). Thus in Qabalistic terms, love can be seen to be synonymous with unity, and vice versa.

The method known as notarikon formed sentences from single words by taking each letter as the initial of a different word. There was also a reverse notarikon by which a sentence could be condensed into a single word by taking only the initial or final letter of each component word. An example of this is the divine name AGLA, often found in magical texts, which stands for *Aieth Gadol Leolam Adonai* (Adonai will be great to eternity). Adonai (the Lord) was the name that was often substituted for Jehova (JHVH) when the latter came to be regarded as a sacrosanct word whose correct pronunciation was a carefully guarded secret.

The notarikon method was also used to yield the seventy-two divine or angelic names collectively called the Schemhamphorasch. These were taken from verses 19,20 and 21 of *Exodus*, chapter 14, which captured the attention of the Qabalists because each verse consisted of seventy-two letters and because verse 19 contained the words 'The angel of the Lord', suggesting that the angelic names were concealed in the text. The decoding method used by the Qabalists was as follows. They wrote out the first verse from right to left, then the second verse underneath it from left to right and finally the third verse at the bottom from right to left again. This yielded seventy-two vertical columns of three letters each, which they converted into names by adding the endings -al, -el or -iah. Thus, for instance, VHV became Vehuiah, SJT became Sitael, and MHS became Mahasiah.

Temurah is the name given to a variety of permutation procedures. Most of these involve writing out the alphabet in two rows, one above the other, and substituting one letter for another in the series according to a set pattern.

Apart from these decoding methods, another important Qabalistic tool was the glyph known as the Tree of Life. This served both as a description of how the universe came into being and as a map of its basic forces and structure. The Qabalist postulates that God created, or rather continually creates, the universe through a series of progressively dense emanations which are arranged into ten stages or modes known as Sephiroth. It is perhaps easiest to think of these as lights. The highest one, Kether, is a concentration of pure divine essence. It remains part of the supreme nothingness, yet contains within it all the lower Sephiroth, just as white light contains all other colours of the spectrum. Kether, by contemplating itself, gives rise to the second light, Hockmah, which is the first active or causal principle in the universe and is also known as the Father. Next comes Binah, the Mother, the receptive, form-giving principle. These three form the Supernal Triad. They cannot be directly perceived by man and are separated from the remainder of the Tree by what is known as the Abyss. The names of the remaining Sephiroth, in descending order, are Chesed or Gedulah (Mercy), Gevurah or Din (Severity), Tiphereth (Beauty), Netzach (Victory), Hod (Splendour), Jesod (the Foundation) and Malkuth (the Kingdom). These ten Sephiroth form ten modes of being which run right through creation, from the universe itself down to the tiniest organism. In the eyes of the Qabalist these ten modes are visible everywhere, always interacting in the same way. The Tree also has something known as Daath (Knowledge), which is usually shown as a point placed in the middle of the Abyss but which really pervades the whole Tree. This refers to the all-pervasive consciousness of God which flows through and illumines all of the Sephiroth. It is the Oneness that remains present in separateness.

The Sephiroth are usually arranged in three triangles with the lone Sephirah Malkuth at the bottom. They can also be seen as being grouped into three 'pillars': a right-hand, masculine 'pillar of force'; a left-hand, feminine 'pillar of form'; and a central, moderating 'pillar of balance'.

The Sephiroth are, to the Qabalist, ten departments of a vast civil service, each of which contains its divisions and subdivisions. Each of these groupings has its powers, its responsibilities, its functions and hierarchy of staff. At the top of each stands a divine name, under which is ranged an archangel, angels and a vast number of demons. Thus, the Tree of Life provides a diagram of the command structure of the invisible bureaucracy of angels and demons, a diagram which is an invaluable guide to the Qabalistic magician when he wishes to summon any part of the bureaucracy to his aid.

And who are the members of this bureaucracy? To draw up a complete list of them would be virtually impossible, for their number runs into many thousands. 'My name is Legion, for we are many', as the evil spirit told Jesus in the New Testament (Mark 5:9). As the grimoires drew on many traditions the ranks of this supernatural hierarchy included gods and demons from the Chaldean, ancient Egyptian, Hellenic, Gnostic and Hebrew religions. From the Egyptians came the concept of the 'decans', the three degrees into which each sign of the zodiac was divided, making thirty-six in all. Each of these decans was ruled by a demon who plagued the part of the body to which his decan corresponded. At the same time each could be counteracted by the invoking of the appropriate angel. For example, in the *Testament of Solomon*, we read:

> The third said: 'I am called *Arôtosael*. I do harm to eyes, and grievously injure them. Only let me hear the words, "*Uriel*, imprison *Aratosael*" [*sic*], at once I retreat' ...
>
> The sixth said: 'I am called *Sphendonaêl*. I cause tumours of the parotid gland, and inflammations of the tonsils, and tetanic recurvation. If I hear, "*Sabrael*, imprison *Sphendonaêl*", at once I retreat' ...
>
> And the ninth said: 'I am called *Kurtaêl*. I send colics in the bowels. I induce pains. If I hear the words, "*Iaôth*, imprison *Kurtaêl*", I at once retreat' ...
>
> The twelfth said: 'I am called *Saphathoraêl*, and I inspire partisanship in men, and delight in causing them to stumble. If any one will write on paper these names of angels, *Iaeô*,

> *Iealô, Iôelet, Sabaôth, Ithoth, Bae,* and having folded it up, wear it round his neck or against his ear, I at once retreat and dissipate the drunken fit ...
>
> The sixteenth said: 'I am called *Atrax*. I inflict upon men fevers, irremediable and harmful. If you would imprison me, chop up coriander and smear it on the lips reciting the following charm: "The fever which is from dirt. I exorcise thee by the throne of the most high God, retreat from dirt and retreat from the creature fashioned by God." And at once I retreat' ... [4]

In due course we shall come across many more names from this Kafkaesque civil service with its labryinth of departments and its strange rules and formalities.[5]

By now it will be apparent that the world of the grimoire is a complex one, full of hazards. But the magician who masters its laws can use his power to many different ends, good and bad. He can use it for healing, foreseeing the future, discovering treasure, striking down his enemies and gaining spiritual enlightenment. Through the ages we find magic being used for all of these purposes and many more.

3.
Early Magical Texts

The grimoires of antiquity were for the most part written on scrolls made from the Egyptian water reed known as papyrus. Strips of the stem were laid to form a mat and them crushed together, producing a loose-textured, porous paper. It was not until Napoleon's invasion of Egypt that significant numbers of these papyri came to light, but by the late nineteenth century the study of them had become sufficiently important to merit the term 'papyrology'.

Although Graeco-Egyptian magic goes back much earlier, most of the magical papyri that have been discovered date from between the third and fifth centuries AD. It was probably a collection of books of this kind that were burnt at Ephesus in Asia Minor by the magicians who had been converted by Saint Paul. As chapter 19 of the *Acts of the Apostles* relates: 'And a good many of those who formerly practised magic collected their books and burnt them publicly. The total value was reckoned up, and it came to fifty thousand pieces of silver.'

A valuable collection of these texts is Karl Preisendanz's *Papyri graecae magicae.* One of the texts reproduced by Preisendanz, the Louvre papyrus, contains an invocation to Helios, the Sun god. This gives a flavour of the higher type of magic and is couched in poetic terms. It reads:

> Come to me, greatest in heaven, for whom the heaven has become a dancing-place [magical words followed by a Coptic word], perform such and such [magical words], you who are the friend of oracles, golden of countenance, glistening with gold, gleaming with fire in the night, mighty, mighty lord of

> the worlds, you who shine forth early in the day, who go down in the western heaven, who rise from the east, who are shaped like a circle, who speed towards midday and linger in Arabia [magical words], herald of the holy light, circle in fiery form [magical words], brilliant Sun, shining over the whole world, covering the ocean [magical words], I beseech you by the egg. I am Adam, the first born, my name is Adam ...[1]

An example of the more debased form of magic is the following love spell from S. Eitrem's collection, *Papyri Osloenses:*

> Write with a bronze stilus on an unbaked potsherd: 'Hecate, you, Hecate of three shapes, all the magical signs of every one having been completed, I adjure you by the great name of Ablathana and the power of Agramari, for I adjure you, you, who control the fire of the Hawk and those in it, that [feminine name], be consumed, and to pursue (her) to me [masculine name], because I hold in my right hand the two serpents and the victory of Iao Sabaoth, and by the great name Bilkatrimopheche, shaking the fire, Stoutoukatatoutou, for her enflamed to love me, in fire for me, yes tortured. Sunkoutouel am I.' Write 8 magical signs, so; give me the favour of all things, Adonai.

The same papyrus contains the following (somewhat confusing) instructions for performing a curse:

> You take a plate of lead and write on it with a bronze stilus the following names and the figure. You anoint the plate with the blood of a bat and roll it up in the usual way; you open a frog (toad), and put it (the plate) into its stomach, sew up the frog with Anubis-thread and a bronze needle and suspend it on a reed taken from the spot with hairs from the tail of a black ox with its hind-legs (tied to the reed) in the eastern part of the place near to the rising sun.
>
> Osirisesengenbarpharanges. [This complex is written in the shape of a heart by cutting off the letters successively from each end.] Erikisephearararacharaephthisikera. Rikisephthearacharaephthisike. Base. Lord angels, as this frog vanishes away and dries up, so may also the body of [masculine name], born of [feminine name], because I adjure you who are placed to command the fire, Maskelli, Maskello, and the rest ...[2]

As B.R. Rees points out, in his article on magical papyri in *Man, Myth and Magic,* these texts evince a great mixture of ingredients from different religious traditions. Greek, Egyptian, Gnostic and Hebrew fragments, as well as other elements, are often found jumbled together. One of these texts, the Berlin papyrus, which appears in Preisendanz's first volume, contains within a short space the names: Apollo, Paieon, Iao, Michael, Gabriel, Abrasax, Adonai, Pakenbeth (for Seth-Typhon), Aion, Physis, Adonaios and Eloaios (for Elohim). Christian references also occur but are comparatively rare, as Christians of that era were normally hostile to magic, with its polytheistic basis. It was only later, with the development of a Christian demonology, that a framework emerged within which a form of Christian magic could exist, albeit uneasily.

In the ancient world there were certain places where magic thrived particularly luxuriantly. For the higher reaches of occult learning there was Alexandria. For folk magic there was Thessaly, a region of Greece where witches abounded. Thessaly features in one of the most vivid fictional accounts of magic in the classical world, namely *The Golden Ass,* by Lucius Apuleius.

The author came from a well-to-do family living in north Africa in the second century AD. He studied at the universities of Carthage and Athens, travelled widely, became initiated into the mysteries of Isis and settled down to a career as a barrister. The story of *The Golden Ass* is to some extent autobiographical. During a visit to Thessaly, the hero (who bears the author's name) has a bout of debauchery with a slave girl and then attempts to turn himself into an owl by means of a magical ointment which the girl gives him. The disastrous results are described as follows:

> After I had rubbed every part and member of my body, I hovered with my arms, and moved myself, looking still to be changed into a bird ... Behold, neither feathers nor appearance of feathers did burgeon out, but verily my hair did turn into ruggedness, and my tender skin waxed tough and hard, my fingers and toes, losing the number of five, changed into hoofs, and out of my arse grew a great tail ... I perceived that I was no bird but a plain ass.[3]

After a series of unpleasant adventures in this form, Lucius is restored to human form by eating some roses during a procession in honour of Isis, and afterwards he is initiated into the Isis cult. The passage describing his initiation is one of great beauty, and the whole story brings out the contrast between debased forms of magic and the true magic of initiation.

The indigenous magic of Greece and Italy was a comparatively simple folk tradition involving spells to control nature, love charms, rejuvenating mixtures and the like. Adepts of these arts were somewhat looked down upon. But with the arrival of the oriental religions the magician began to gain in status. 'Until the end of paganism', writes Cumont, 'magic and religion in Rome remained so closely associated that it is sometimes difficult to distinguish the texts of one from those of the other.' However, Cumont also points out that the ancients expressly distinguished 'magic', which was always under suspicion and disapproved of, from the legitimate and honourable art for which the name 'theurgy' was invented. Those who practised the more disreputable forms were subject to severe penalties, and even the simple fact of possessing books of sorcery made one liable to prosecution.

When Christianity was adopted by the Roman empire, magic was ever more fiercely condemned, but still it continued to thrive. The old religions died away, but their magical practices lived on. An instance of this survival is an occurrence that took place towards the end of the fifth century at Beirut. As Cumont describes it:

> One night some students of the famous law-school of that city attempted to kill a slave in the circus to aid the master in obtaining the favour of a woman who scorned him. Being reported, they had to deliver up their hidden volumes, of which those of Zoroaster and of Hostanes were found, together with those written by the astrologer Manetho. The whole city was agitated, and searches proved that many young men preferred the study of the illicit science to that of Roman law. By order of the bishop a solemn auto-da-fé was made of all this literature, in the presence of the city officials and the clergy, and the most revolting passages were read in

public 'in order to acquaint everybody with the conceited and vain promises of the demons', as the pious writer of the story says.[4]

As Christianity tightened its hold on Europe, many more 'forbidden' books were burned, and their owners too were often consigned to the flames. Under this persecution, magic suffered an eclipse, and magical books became scarce, though the occult arts never died away completely. Meanwhile magic was kept alive in the Semitic world, by both Arab and Jewish practitioners, and around the twelfth century magical texts began to penetrate Christian Europe once again, coming from Muslim Spain along with Arabic scientific writings. One of the most important and seminal of these Arabic treatises was the *Picatrix,* to use the title given to its Latin version. Recent research has revealed that this is a translation of an Arabic book called *The Aim of the Sage,* doubtfully attributed to one al-Maggriti (meaning 'the man from Madrid'), a mathematician of Arab Spain who lived in about the twelfth century AD. A Spanish translation was made for King Alfonso of Castile in 1256 and later the book was translated into Latin. Thereafter it circulated widely in manuscript. There was one copy in the library of the German Kaiser Maximilian (1459-1519). The occultists Pietro d'Abano and Cornelius Agrippa used it, and it was widely quoted in literature. In 1456 Johann Hartlieb, physician to the Margrave of Brandenburg, warned his royal master against the *Picatrix,* calling it 'a remarkable example of necromantic literature' which 'leads many people to eternal damnation'.[5] Rabelais refers to the author of the *Picatrix* in his *Pantagruel,* where he claims that when he studied at Toledo he was taught by the 'Reverend Father in the Devil, Piccatrix, doctor of the faculty of diabolism'

The subsequent history of the *Picatrix* illustrates the curious law which appears to protect any tradition of sufficient power. Even if that tradition is recorded on only one piece of parchment buried in the ground in some remote spot, it seems to be the case that the gods will ensure that the parchment is dug up and brought to public attention when history is ready for it. Perhaps it is this law that lies behind the idea that certain grimoires can never be destroyed or lost by their owners.

As for the *Picatrix*, it survived the attempts of the Church to eradicate magical literature, but fell victim to the eighteenth-century Enlightenment and remained in obscurity until the 1920s when it aroused the interest of two German scholars, Helmut Ritter and Martin Plessner, who translated it into German in the summer of 1929 while staying at Ritter's house in Constantinople. The Leipzig printing firm of Teubner started setting up the book in type and running off the printed sheets which were carefully checked by the translators. The work was slowed down when Plessner moved to Haifa, and by the outbreak of the Second World War only a third of the book had been printed in proof. During the war the corrected proofs and all the plates of type were destroyed. Only one copy of the translation survived the war and made its way to England. After being re-worked by Plessner, this was finally published by the Warburg Insititute in 1962.

In his foreword to this edition, G. Bing writes that the *Picatrix* is a 'classic example of the way in which remnants of ancient Greek thought found their way into Arabic cosmology, in alliance with the belief in the sorcerer's art descended from a still remoter antiquity.'[6] This Arabic magical lore, with its hierarchies of angels and demons and its complex network of correspondences, was an important tool in the hands of the various occult brotherhoods of the Middle East. Helmut Ritter writes in his introduction of an encyclopaedia called the Iḫwān al-Safā, which originated in Iraq and was one of the chief sources of the *Picatrix*. This encyclopaedia, he says, 'reflects the outlook of a remarkable philosophical secret society whose members called themselves the 'Faithful Ones' or, more usually, the 'Pure Brethren'. They were related to the Schiite sect which was particularly open to the classical tradition of thought.'[7]

The cosmology of this sect was based on a doctrine of emanations from the ultimate creator, by way of an 'Intellect', then through an 'All-Soul', down through increasingly dense stages of manifestation to material creation. The all-soul, according to this belief, had two powers, one of knowledge and the other of action; and these two powers affected all bodies and gave them their character.

The following prayer to the presiding deity of the planet Jupiter gives an idea of the flavour of the *Picatrix*:

> O Rūfijā'il, thou angel who art set over Jupiter, thou blessed, perfect, complete and divine master, thou of beautiful raiment, dignity and wisdom, far from all evil and unclean speech! I call thee by all thy names: in Arabic, o Muštari; in Persian, o Birğis; in Iranian, o Hormuz; in Greek, o Zeus; in Indian, o Wihasfati.[8]

For those who which to make doubly sure of Jupiter's aid, there are also instructions for making a Jupiter talisman:

> Engrave on a white corundum stone the image of a man with a crown on his head, on a throne with four feet, each one resting on the neck of a man standing. These men are winged, and the figure on the throne has his hand raised. Do this in the hour and exaltation of the planet. Result: increase in prestige and prosperity for the wearer.[9]

By emphasizing such passages as the above it is easy to overlook the fact that the *Picatrix* is much more than just a manual of magical formulae. Behind it is a lofty mystical philosophy characterized by a gnostic outlook and incorporating many ideas from the Hermeticism of the Hellenistic world. Hermeticism, which will be discussed in greater detail in Chapter 5, was a movement which arose in Hellenistic Egypt in the first and second centuries AD and subsequently disappeared underground for many centuries. We tend to credit the men of the Italian Renaissance with having rediscovered Hermeticism in the fifteenth century. But in fact, as in many other areas, the Muslims got there first. As early as the twelfth century AD men like the great Persian mystic Sohravardi were evolving a remarkable synthesis of Hermeticism, Zoroastrianism, Neoplatonism and Islamic Sufism, as well as other elements. It is this synthesis that lies behind the *Picatrix*, and it is worth examining some of its main features as described in Henry Corbin's fascinating book *The Man of Light in Iranian Sufism.*[10]

Central to this Hermetic-Sufi gnosis was the notion that each person has a heavenly 'guide of light', also referred to as 'Perfect Nature', who is both the individual's own higher self and an angel of God. At the same time each man has, within his dense physical being, an entity of finer substance known as the 'man of light'. It is only through the man of light within him that he can communicate with the guide of light, or Perfect Nature and thus attain spiritual enlightenment. In order for us to achieve this goal it is necessary for us to banish our mundane 'daylight' consciousness and reach a dark centre within ourselves which can then be illuminated by the pure inner light bestowed by Perfect Nature. This moment of inner illumination is described in the following remarkable passage in the *Picatrix:*

> When I wished to bring to light the science of the mystery and nature of Creation, I came upon a subterranean vault full of darkness and winds. I could see nothing because of the darkness, nor could I keep any lamp alight because of the many winds. Then a person appeared to me in my sleep in a form of the greatest beauty. He said to me: 'Take a lamp and place it under a glass to shield it from the winds: then it will give thee light in spite of them. Then go into the vault; dig in its centre and from there bring forth a certain talismanic image, artfully made. When you have drawn out this image, the winds will cease to blow through the vault. Then dig in its four corners and you will bring to light the knowledge of the mysteries of Creation, the causes of Nature, the origins and qualities of things.' At that I said to him: 'Who then art thou?' He replied: 'I am thy Perfect Nature. If thou wishest to see me, call me by my name.'[11]

If the medieval detractors of the *Picatrix* had read such passages carefully and with an open mind they would have discovered that this grimoire in fact contains a mystical teaching of great beauty. But three centuries had to pass after its appearance before Europe was ready for a large-scale revival of Hermeticism.

4.

All Solomon's Wisdom

The history of magical literature abounds in dubious claims as to the authorship of texts. Often a text would be ascribed to a famous or legendary figure or to a name which simply had an exotic ring about it. And once a name had become fashionable the texts attributed to it multiplied rapidly. Thus it is possible to distinguish whole 'families' of texts, each of which has an attribution and certain features in common, though of course these families often interbreed and overlap. We find, for example, a Solomonic family, an Orphic family, a Hermetic family and numerous others. Of these, the Solomonic family is probably the largest.

Solomon (c.973-933BC), third King of Israel and builder of the great Temple at Jerusalem, is a figure whose name is associated not only with wisdom and splendour, but also with the power to control the spirits of the invisible world. Both Jewish and Muslim literature credit him with miraculous powers. It is difficult to establish when his reputation as a magician originated, but the Jewish historian, Flavius Josephus, writing in the first century AD, affirms the existence of a grimoire written by Solomon and describes how devils were conjured up with the aid of this book. Whether Solomon himself ever wrote such a book is open to doubt, but it is clear that behind the Solomonic literature is a Qabalistic magical system of great antiquity, even though the system has been greatly debased in the countless pseudo-Solomonic grimoires.

It is not surprising to find that the hexagram or Star of David, familiar as the emblem of the state of Israel and also as a magical sigil, is also referred to as the Seal of Solomon (confusingly, the names Star of David and Seal of Solomon are also frequently used to refer to the pentagram). In an essay on the history of this symbol, Gershom Scholem writes:

> The seal of Solomon is manifestly connected with the legend ... concerning Solomon's dominion over the spirits. This legend also speaks of a signet ring on which originally, to be sure, was engraved not a magic emblem but the ineffable name of God, the tetragrammaton. The power of this signet ring is described with great aplomb in texts of Jewish — and later also Christian — magic, such as the *Testament of Solomon,* a Greek manual of Jewish and Judaeo-Christian Magic which in its original elements is very old. As yet we cannot say for sure when the inscription on this wondrous signet ring was replaced by one of the two figures. We only know this much for certain: It happened before the sixth century, i.e., before the rise of Islam.[1]

The importance of the Solomonic literature is shown by the numerous references to it, both respectful and hostile, among writers from Josephus onwards. Thorndike writes:

> In the first half of the thirteenth century William of Auvergne, bishop of Paris, in his treatise on laws declares that there is no divinity in the angles of Solomon's pentagon, that the rings of Solomon and the seals of Solomon and nine candles (*candariae*) are a form of idolatry, and involve execrable consecrations and detestable invocations and images ... Some years later Albertus Magnus, listing evil books of necromantic images in his *Speculum astronomiae,* includes five treatises current under the name of Solomon, and seems to have in mind about the same works as William.[2]

The opposition of the Church to the Solomonic literature was fierce. In about 1350 a book entitled *Le Livre de Salomon,* dealing with the invocation of demons, was burned on the orders of Pope Innocent VI, and in 1559 the Roman Inquisition prohibited the *Key of Solomon* as a dangerous work. The *Key* was also one of the works warned against by Johann Hartlieb in his pamphlet on undesirable literature written for the Margrave of Brandenburg in 1456.

But the mystique surrounding the name of Solomon was proof against the strongest prosecution, and the Solomonic books, chiefly the *Key* and its many variations, continued to proliferate. E.M. Butler, in her book *Ritual Magic*, points out that the bulk of these texts remained in manuscript form even after the invention of printing in the fifteenth century.

> Their great rarity in print is not due entirely to fear of desecration, nor to fear of prosecution, although both may well have played ... a part ... But the real deterrent lies in the fact that printed texts are useless. They must be copied out by the exorcist himself with a consecrated pen on consecrated paper; and more confidence has generally been felt in making such copies from the personal manuscript of a magician of repute than from printed texts, whose origin must always be extremely doubtful. The forgery of magical manuscripts has therefore naturally figured as a remunerative side-line of the industry. There are many manuscripts of the *Key of Solomon* in the great libraries; there are probably hundreds in private collections and in the possession of individuals all over Europe. In 1903 Hermann Gollancz described a Hebrew version in his possession and published a facsimile of it in 1914 with an introduction and a table of contents, also quoting from it at length. He dated it 1700 or thereabouts, and believed that it was copied from an older version. He vouched for the 'perfectly Jewish' tone of the prayers, whilst discerning other elements in the conjurations and elsewhere. This particular text differs radically from the one established by Mathers in 1889 from seven codices: one in sixteenth-century Latin, one in Italian and five in French, all in the British Museum.[3]

S.L. MacGregor Mathers is an important figure in this story for others reasons as well. We shall encounter him in a later chapter as one of the most colourful occultists of the nineteenth century. Meanwhile, let me pause here to examine some of the contents of this Solomonic literature.

One of the most important items in Mathers's version of the *Key* as well as in many other grimoires, is a table of planetary hours, a very significant tool in magical work, since every operation should ideally take place on the day and at the hour of the appropriate planet. For example an

6 TABLE OF THE PLANETARY HOURS.

Sunday.	*Monday.*	*Tuesday.*	*Wednes.*	*Hours from Sunset to Sunset.*	*Hours from Midnight to Midnight.*	*Thursd.*	*Friday.*	*Saturd.*
Merc.	Jup.	Ven.	Sat.	8	1	Sun.	Moon.	Mars.
Moon.	Mars.	Mer.	Jup.	9	2	Ven.	Sat.	Sun.
Sat.	Sun.	Moon.	Mars.	10	3	Mer.	Jup.	Ven.
Jup.	Ven.	Sat.	Sun	11	4	Moon.	Mars.	Mer.
Mars.	Mer.	Jup.	Ven.	12	5	Sat.	Sun.	Moon.
Sun.	Moon.	Mars.	Mer.	1	6	Jup.	Ven.	Sat.
Ven.	Sat.	Sun.	Moon.	2	7	Mars.	Mer.	Jup.
Mer.	Jup.	Ven.	Sat.	3	8	Sun.	Moon.	Mars.
Moon.	Mars.	Mer.	Jup.	4	9	Ven.	Sat.	Sun.
Sat.	Sun.	Moon.	Mars.	5	10	Mer.	Jup.	Ven.
Jup.	Ven.	Sat.	Sun.	6	11	Moon.	Mars.	Mer.
Mars.	Mer.	Jup.	Ven.	7	12	Sat.	Sun.	Moon.
Sun.	Moon.	Mars.	Mer.	8	1	Jup.	Ven.	Sat.
Ven.	Sat.	Sun.	Moon.	9	2	Mars.	Mer.	Jup.
Mer.	Jup.	Ven.	Sat.	10	3	Sun.	Moon.	Mars.
Moon.	Mars.	Mer.	Jup.	11	4	Ven.	Sat.	Sun.
Sat.	Sun.	Moon.	Mars.	12	5	Mer.	Jup.	Ven.
Jup.	Ven.	Sat.	Sun.	1	6	Moon.	Mars.	Mer.
Mars.	Mer.	Jup.	Ven.	2	7	Sat.	Sun.	Moon.
Sun.	Moon.	Mars.	Mer.	3	8	Jup.	Ven.	Sat.
Ven.	Sat.	Sun.	Moon.	4	9	Mars.	Mer.	Jup.
Mer.	Jup.	Ven.	Sat.	5	10	Sun.	Moon.	Mars.
Moon.	Mars.	Mer.	Jup.	6	11	Ven.	Sat.	Sun.
Sat.	Sun.	Moon.	Mars.	7	12	Mer.	Jup.	Ven.

operation to find a lost book would come under the auspices of Mercury as the god of writing, love spells would come under Venus, and so on. To find the right day is easy. Saturday, Sunday and Monday are obviously governed by Saturn, Sun and Moon. For the other days (named in English after Norse gods) one only needs to remember the French names to know their planetary attributions: Mardi (Tuesday), Mars; Mercredi (Wednesday), Mercury; Jeudi (Thursday), Jupiter; Vendredi (Friday), Venus. The sequence of hours is based on the order of the planets on the Qabalistic Tree of Life, which in turn is based on the ancient geocentric universe. Emanating out from the earth are Moon, Mercury, Venus, Sun, Mars, Jupiter and Saturn. In the planetary tables they are taken in the reverse order. The day is divided into two halves: sunrise to sunset, and sunset to sunrise. Each of these is divided into twelve 'hours'. But obviously it is only at the equinoxes that the daylight hours will be of the same length as the night-time ones. In summer the daylight hours will be longer than those after dark, and in winter vice-versa.

The first hour after sunrise is ruled by the planet of the

day, and each subsequent hour is ruled by each of the other planets in rotation. Following the sequence through to the next day, it will be found that the first hour after sunrise falls on the appropriate planet (see accompanying table). Given the order of the planets, and given a twenty-four-hour day and a seven-day week, the system will work only if the days are in the order that we know them. So we can assume that the ancient Egyptians, who named the days after the planets, did so in order to make the planetary tables work. This is another proof that the basic ingredients of the grimoires are of great antiquity, even though they often contain more recent material.

At first sight the system of planetary hours seems highly irrational, even in astrological terms. What possible relation can the third hour of daylight on a Tuesday have to the planet Venus? We have to remember, however, that the reason for following a set of instructions in a grimoire has very often to do with the side-effects on the magician himself as he carries out the procedure. In order to operate the planetary tables he must rise early enough to know the exact time of sunrise, and he must then divide the hours of daylight into twelve precise compartments. Calculating the exact length of these compartments in, say, July, would be no easy task, especially in an age when there were no precise clocks. Thus the whole procedure encourages discipline and accurate observation.

The Mathers edition of the *Greater Key of Solomon* explains that there are two kinds of magical operation: those that require a magical circle and those that do not. In the case of the former, a complex and rigorous series of preparations is necessary, as the grimoire explains:

> Before commencing the operations both the Master and his Disciples must abstain with great and thorough continence during the space of nine days from sensual pleasures and from vain and foolish conversation ... Six of these nine days having expired, he must recite frequently the Prayer and Confession as will be told him; and on the Seventh Day, the Master being alone, let him enter into a secret place, let him take off his clothes, and bathe himself from head to foot in consecrated and exorcised Water, saying devoutly and humbly the prayer, 'O Lord Adonaï,' etc. ...

The Prayer being finished, let the Master quit the water, and put upon his flesh raiment of white linen clean and unsoiled; and then let him go with his Disciples unto a secret place and command them to strip themselves naked; and they having taken off their clothes, let him take exorcised water and pour it upon their heads so that it flows down to their feet and bathes them completely; and while pouring this water upon them let the Master say: 'Be ye regenerate, renewed, washed, and pure,' etc. ...

Which being done, the Disciples must clothe themselves, putting upon their flesh, like their Master, raiment of white linen clean and unsoiled; and the last three days the Master and his Disciples should fast, observing the solemnities and prayers ...

After the preliminaries have been completed, the Master issues magical weapons, which are carried by the disciples in a special order. The text continues:

The First Disciple will bear the Censer, the Perfumes and the Spices; the Second Disciple will bear the Book, Papers, Pens, Ink and any stinking or impure materials; the Third will carry the Knife and the Sickle of Magical Art, the Lantern, and the Candles; the Fourth, the Psalms and the rest of the Instruments; the Fifth, the Crucible or Chafing-dish, and the Charcoal or Fuel; but it is necessary for the Master himself to carry in his hand the Staff and the Wand or Rod. The things necessary being thus disposed, the Master will go with his Disciples unto the assigned place, where they have proposed to construct the Circle for the Magical Arts and experiments ...

When the Master shall have arrived at the place appointed, together with his Disciples, he having lighted the flame of the fire, and having exorcised it afresh ... shall light the Candle and place it in the Lantern, which one of the Disciples is to hold ever in his hand to light the Master at his work. Now the Master of the Art, every time that he shall have occasion for some particular purpose to speak with the Spirits, must endeavour to form certain Circles which shall differ somewhat, and shall have some particular reference to the particular experiment under consideration.

There then follow instructions for making the circle:

Take thou the Knife, the Sickle, or the Sword of Magical Art ... With this Knife or with this Sickle of Art thou shalt describe, beyond the inner Circle which thou shalt have already formed, a Second Circle, encompassing the other at the distance of one foot therefrom and having the same centre. Within this space of a foot in breadth between the first and second circumferential line, thou shalt trace towards the Four Quarters of the Earth, the Sacred and Venerable Symbols of the holy letter Tau. And between the first and the second Circle, which thou shalt thyself have drawn with the Instrument of Magical Art, thou shalt make four hexagonal pentacles, and between these thou shalt write four terrible and tremendous Names of God, viz.:

Between the East and the South the Supreme Name IHVH, Tetragrammaton;

Between the South and the West the Essential Tetragrammatic Name AHIH, Eheieh;

Between the West and the North the Name of Power ALIVN, Elion;

And between the North and the East the Great Name ALH, Eloah;

Which Names are of supreme importance in the list of the Sephiroth, and their Sovereign Equivalents.

Furthermore, thou shalt circumscribe about these Circles two Squares, the Angles of which shall be turned towards the Four Quarters of the Earth; and the space between the Lines of Outer and Inner Square shall be half-a-foot. The extreme Angles of the Outer Square shall be made the Centres of four Circles, the measure or diameter of which shall be one foot. All these are to be drawn with the Knife or consecrated Instrument of Art. And within these Four Circles thou must write these four Names of God the Most Holy One, in this order:

At the East. AL. El;
At the West, IH, Yah;
At the South, AGLA, Agla;
And at the North, ADNI, Adonaï.

Having lit a censer in each of the four outer circles, the Master enters the inner circle, closes it magically and then says:

When we enter herein with all humility, let God the Almighty One enter into this Circle, by the entrance of an

> eternal happiness, of a Divine prosperity, of a perfect joy, of an abundant charity, and of an eternal salutation. Let all the demons fly from this place, especially those who are opposed unto this work, and let the Angels of Peace assist and protect this Circle, from which let discord and strife fly and depart. Magnify and extend upon us, O Lord, Thy most Holy Name, and bless our conversation and our assembly. Sanctify, O Lord our God, our humble entry herein, Thou the Blessed and Holy one of the Eternal Ages! Amen.

He then kneels down and recites a prayer:

> O Lord God, All Powerful and All Merciful, Thou Who desirest not the death of a sinner, but rather that he may turn from his wickedness and live; give and grant unto us thy grace, by blessing and consecrating this earth and this circle, which is here marked out with the most powerful and holy Names of God ...
>
> I beseech Thee, O Lord God, the All Powerful and the All Merciful, that Thou wilt deign to bless this Circle, and all this place, and all those who are therein, and that Thou wilt grant unto us, who serve thee, and rehearse nothing but the wonders of Thy law, a good Angel for our Guardian; remove from us every adverse power; preserve us from evil and from trouble; grant, O Lord, that we may rest in this place in all safety through Thee, O Lord, Who livest and reignest unto the Ages of the Ages. Amen.[4]

The procedure described here contains basic patterns that tend to crop up wherever ritual of a transcendental nature is worked. The ceremonial framework of the four cardinal points is used, for example, in Freemasonry, but without the theurgic ingredient. Parallels can also be found outside the European tradition in, for instance, the ceremonies of the Navaho Indians of the south-western United States, who use the four quarters in their healing rituals.

When we examine the working from the *Key of Solomon*, which has just been quoted, we see that it can be used, like other occult and magical systems, to bring about a state of wholeness by linking the mundane and divine spheres and by uniting the disparate elements in the magician himself so that he is guided by his 'Guardian Angel', that is to say his higher self.

In the floor tracing used in the ritual, the squares represent the mundane sphere and the circles represent the divine. The mundane realm is thus bounded by the divine, through the four small circles at the quarters. But the divine lies also at the centre of the mundane; hence the three circles within the two squares. The diagram bears a striking resemblance to certain oriental mandalas, which often take the form of a series of concentric circles within a square. The Tantric variety sometimes features in the centre the image of the god Shiva in intercourse with his consort Shakti, an emblem of unification or wholeness. The working circle of the magician can therefore be seen as a western form of the mandala. The parallel is made clear by Benjamin Walker, who writes:

> The word *mandala* means a circle and in Hindu and Buddhist rites is applied to a diagram traced on the ground or painted on a board or piece of fabric, symbolizing the cosmic and heavenly regions. Properly drawn and duly consecrated it becomes a focus of occult energy, drawing down hidden powers and itself sending forth magical emanations like a talisman. In its simplest form it is circular in outline but any symmetrical figure such as a square, pentagon, star or floral shape can be used. The outer perimeter is meant to delineate the mandala's borders, to act as a protective barrier against outside intrusion and to confine the power engendered inside the enclosure ...
>
> In one form or another the mandala is found in almost every culture in the world. It is an archetype of holy ground, a round and hence 'perfect' zone, set aside as sacroscanct ...
>
> In Western occultism its analogue is the magic circle whose exact demarcations are given in medieval grimoires. The difference between the two is that after the magic circle is drawn the Western magician steps inside its protective boundaries so that the spirits he summons cannot invade his territory to molest him, whereas the Eastern practitioner remains outside the mandala while the spirit powers remain within.[5]

When we come to some of the spells in the *Key of Solomon* used for specific purposes, such as making oneself invisible, finding treasure or obtaining favours in love, it might seem that the tone of the book has become lower.

But we must remember that magic is not just a spiritual discipline. It is also intended to be a means of achieving practical aims through the fortifying of the will. But the complex procedures given in the *Key* and in other grimoires are also a test of the will.

Take, for example, the making of pentacles or talismans, one of the favourite means of attaining a specific end by magical means. Part of the chapter on pentacles reads as follows:

> These Pentacles are usually made of the metal the most suitable to the nature of the Planet ... They should be engraved with the instrument of Art in the days and hours proper to the Planet.
>
> Saturn ruleth over Lead; Jupiter over Tin; Mars over Iron; the Sun over Gold; Venus over Copper; Mercury over the mixture of Metals; more often Mercury is attributed to quicksilver; and the Moon over Silver.
>
> They may also be made with exorcised virgin paper, writing thereon with the colours adopted for each Planet ... and according to the Planet with which the Pentacle is in sympathy ...
>
> The Matter of which the Pentacle is constructed should be virgin, never having been used for any other purpose; or if it be metal it should be purified by fire.
>
> As regards the size of the Pentacles it is arbitrary, so long as they are made according to the rules, and with the requisite solemnities, as hath been ordained ...
>
> When thou shalt construct these Pentacles and Characters, it is necessary never to forget the burning of Temple Incense, nor to employ anything beyond that of which mention is made.
>
> It is necessary, above all things, to be attentive to the operation, and never to forget or omit those things which contribute to the success which the Pentacles and Experiments promise, having ever in thy mind no other intention than the Glory of God, the accomplishment of thy desires, and loving-kindness towards thy neighbour.[6]

The effect of carrying out a spell or making a talisman, according to such rigorous requirements, would be either to confirm one's will or to cause one to abandon the effort. But there is also a deeper principle at work, which can be seen in many other traditions. It involves starting with an apparently mundane or practical aim and following a set of rigorous procedures in such a way that during the course of the operation the original aim recedes into the background and the practitioner finds himself lifted on to a higher level of consciousness. This is exactly what happens in the Zen Buddhist method of teaching archery. And undoubtedly the same principle is behind many of the grimoires. Through the promise of treasure, love or power, and the titillatingly sinister flavour of the grimoires, the reader finds himself following an arduous discipline to which under normal circumstances he would be unwilling to submit himself. Then, if he perseveres, he finds himself being transformed by the higher and finer energies to which he is exposing himself.

By the same token, of course, the magician may find himself exposed to lower, diabolic energies. Or he may over-inflate part of his own character and set up an imbalance in himself. This is particularly likely to happen if he is using one of the debased grimoires which are so often purveyed under the name of Solomon.

These pseudo-Solomonic grimoires vary greatly in content. Very different from the version quoted earlier in this chapter is a German *Key of Solomon*, published in the year 1686, whose title page bears a sort of demonic *imprimatur*: 'by dispensation of the spirit Aratron'. The text is preceded by the following preamble:

> We Aratron, Bethor, Phaleg, Och, Hagith, Opiel and Phul, ruling spirits above and below the earth, true possessors of its wealth, do hereby command all persons, if they wish to avoid our disfavour, in no way to alter, falsify or extend this revelation of our secret. Whoever infringes this law will be banished to the realm of Pluto.

Possibly this was the text that Goethe had in mind when he portrayed Faust using a Solomonic grimoire. It contains no talismans or magical circles but is basically a manual for summoning spirits.

It will be apparent that the Solomonic literature covers an immense variety of material, some of it belonging to a high mystical and magical tradition, some of an altogether lower order. The disciple of Solomon must therefore be careful to separate the wheat from the chaff.

5.
OTHER NAMES TO CONJURE WITH

Turning to other families of magical texts, we find a small but significant group attributed to Orpheus, who, in Greek mythology, was the son of Apollo and Calliope. He could play the lyre so beautifully that even the rocks were affected. The most familiar story connected with him is that of his attempt to rescue his wife Eurydice from Hades. In the ancient world Orpheus was the focus of a great mystery cult, and it is not surprising that he is credited with having written magical works. One of them is a poem, still extant, of some seven hundred and seventy lines, entitled *Lithica* and dating from around the fourth century AD. This sets out the virtues of some thirty gems (hence the title, from the Greek *lithos*, stone) and also makes allusion to magical practices. Thorndike summarizes the book as follows:

> The *Lithica* opens by representing Hermes as bestowing upon mankind the precious lore, the marvelous virtues of gems. In his cave are stored stones which banish ghosts, robbers and snakes, which bring health, happiness, victory in war and games, honor at courts and success in love, and which insure safety on journeys, the favor of the gods, and enable one to read the hidden thoughts of others and to understand the language of the birds as they predict the future. Few persons, however, avail themselves of this mystic lore, and those who do so are liable to be executed on the charge of magic. After this introduction, which may be regarded as a piquant appetizer to whet the reader's taste for further details, the virtues of individual stones are described, first in the words of Theodamas, a wise and divine man whom the author meets on his way to perform animal sacrifice at an altar of the

> Sun ... and then in a speech of the seer Helenus to Philoctetes which Theodamas quotes.[1]

Hermes, mentioned as the father of this lore of gems, is an even more important figure in this story, rivalling even Solomon in the number of works attributed to him. He began as the Greek god Hermes (known to the Romans as Mercury) and later became identified with the Egyptian god Thoth, inventor of writing. In the hands of classical writers he began to assume the character of an actual historical person, a semi-divine seer who gave the world knowledge of the occult sciences. To this mysterious figure, often called Hermes Trismegistus (the 'Thrice Great') was attributed a vast literature in Greek which emerged out of the Gnostic melting-pot of Egypt around the first and second centuries AD. As Frances Yates points out, this Hermetic literature divides into two branches:

> On the one hand there are the philosophical treatises, such as those in the *Corpus Hermeticum*, and the *Asclepius* ... On the other hand there is the astrological, alchemical, and magical literature, much of which also went under the name of Hermes Trismegistus. These two branches cannot be kept entirely separate from one another ... Gnosticism and magic go together. The pessimist gnostic needs to know the magical words and signs by which he may rid himself of the evil material power of the stars in his upward ascent through the spheres. The optimist gnostic has no fear to draw down by sympathetic magic, invocations, talismans, those same powers of the universe which he believes to be good.
>
> The methods of sympathetic magic presuppose that continual effluvia of influences pouring down onto earth from the stars of which the author of the *Asclepius* speaks. It was believed that these effluvia and influences could be canalised and used by an operator with the requisite knowledge ... The operator who wished to capture, let us say, the power of the planet Venus, must know what plants belonged to Venus, what stones and metals, what animals, and use only these when addressing Venus ... The methods and the cosmological background presupposed are the same whether the magician is using these forces to try to obtain concrete material benefits for himself, or whether he is using them religiously, as in the hieratic magic described in the *Asclepius*.[2]

Frances Yates goes on to point out that the Hermetic writings, with their background of Hellenistic astrology, also absorbed an Egyptian element, namely the thirty-six decans, that is to say the gods ruling over the thirty-six divisions of ten degrees each, making up the zodiacal circle of three hundred and sixty degrees. Each sign of the zodiac thus had three decans as its three 'faces', but the decans were also powerful deities in their own right, taken from the Egyptian pantheon, and each decan had its image.

The reputation of Hermes as a great sage can be judged from the number of references to him among classical and Christian writers. Thorndike writes:

> Our two chief descriptions of the Hermetic books from the period of the Roman Empire are found in the *Stromata* of the Christian Clement of Alexandria (c. AD 150–220) and in the *De Mysteriis* ascribed to the Neo-Platonist Iamblichus (died about AD 330) ... Iamblichus repeats the statement of Seleucus that Hermes wrote twenty thousand volumes and the assertion of Manetho that there were 36,525 books, a number doubtless connected with the supposed length of the year, three hundred and sixty-five and one-quarter days. Iamblichus adds that Hermes wrote one hundred treatises on the ethereal gods and one thousand concerning the celestial gods. He is aware, however, that most books attributed to Hermes were not really composed by him, since in other passages he speaks of 'the books which are circulated under the name of Hermes,' and explains that 'our ancestors ... inscribed all their own writings with the name of Hermes,' thus dedicating them to him as the patron deity of language and theology.[3]

The third-century Christian writer Lactantius took a positive view of Hermes. In his *Institutes* he writes admiringly of Hermes as one who perceived in advance the truths that were taught by Christianity. He points out Hermes' assertion of existence of one supreme God and quotes his reference to a secondary deity created by the ultimate God and loved by him as his own son.

Augustine, writing in the fourth century, adopted a different view of Hermes, attacking the Hermetic writings as idolatrous and condemning their magical content. Despite Augustine's condemnation, however, many

Christians continued to regard Hermes as a wise precursor of Christ. This view is illustrated in a mosaic pavement in Siena Cathedral showing Hermes flanked by Sibyls holding prophecies of the coming of Christianity.

As mentioned earlier, the Hermetic tradition also penetrated the Arab world. One of the earliest alchemical treatises translated from Arabic into Latin was *The Book of the Composition of Alchemy*. The translation, made in 1144, was the work of an Englishman, Robert of Chester, who, in his preface, gives an account of three Hermeses: Enoch, Noah and the philosopher-king called Hermes Triplex who reigned in Egypt after the flood. It was this Hermes, says Robert, who, after the deluge, brought to light again all the arts and sciences and who first discovered and published the present work. Following Robert's preface comes an account of what happened to the book after that. After the time of Christ a certain Adfar of Alexandria found it and mastered it after long study. He later passed his knowledge of the book on to a Christian named Morienus, who used it to make gold. Its history beyond that point enters the realms of fantasy.

The infiltration of works from the Arab world into Christian Europe included, as we have seen, a certain number of Hermetic writings, but it was in the Renaissance that Hermes really came into his own, as we shall see in a later chapter.

Meanwhile let us turn to some of the other names associated with magical literature. The Persian prophet Zoroaster, for example, vies with Hermes for the title of founder of magic. Books attributed to Zoroaster are found quoted, but none of the texts have survived.

The same is not true of the patriarch Enoch, whose name has been linked with that of Hermes, to the extent that some medieval writers even believed them to be one and the same. The most important of the Enochian writings is the *Book of Enoch*, the surviving remains of a complex of literature attributed to the prophet. The book survived in Greek fragments which were discovered in the nineteenth century in Upper Egypt, and there are also versions in Ethiopic and Slavonic, differing considerably from one another. The New Testament writers were familiar with the *Book of Enoch* and were influenced by it, but after AD 300 it became discredited, except among Ethiopic and Slavonic Christians, probably because of its magical flavour, even though the book explicitly states that magic is evil. To quote Thorndike:

> The Enoch literature has much to say concerning angels, and implies their control of nature, man and the future. We hear of Raphael, 'who is set over all the diseases and wounds of the children of men'; Gabriel, 'who is set over all the powers'; Phanuel, 'who is set over the repentance and hope of those who inherit eternal life.' ... The fallen angels in particular are mentioned in the *Book of Enoch*. Two hundred angels lusted after the comely daughters of men and bound themselves by oaths to marry them. After having thus taken unto themselves wives, they instructed the human race in the art of magic and the science of botany.[4]

The reputation of the Enoch literature was to capture the imaginations of those who aspired to the magical knowledge conferred by the angels. One of these was the English magus John Dee, to whom we shall return later.

Apart from the names that I have mentioned in connection with magical writings, there are others which are less readily identifiable. There are, for example, several works attributed to one Toc, Toc Graecus or Tosgraec. One of these is called the *Book of Venus* or the *Book of the Twelve Stones of Venus*. Thorndike speculates that the name is a corruption of Thoth, the Egyptian equivalent of Hermes. But those who wrote his name on the title pages of grimoires had probably forgotten its derivation and merely thought that it sounded suitably impressive and exotic. One of these grimoires is in the Bibliothèque de l'Arsenal in Paris (No. 2493). It is entitled *Le Secret des Secrets, ou le Véritable Grimoire* (the Secret of Secrets, or the True Grimoire), by Tosgraec, and appears to date from the seventeenth century. The preface to the book purports to have been written by King Solomon, who entrusts the volume to his son Roboam, telling him that no magical work can succeed without it. The text then goes on to explain that the work came into the hands of Tosgraec, 'a certain very learned philosopher'. Tosgraec, in despair at his inability to understand the book, was visited by an angel who agreed to interpret it for him on condition that he did not reveal its secrets to anyone unworthy. The text contains the usual instructions for commanding spirits, making talismans and casting spells for various purposes. The invocations are a mixture of Hebrew, Latin and words that are unidentifiable. Here, for example, is the prayer used as part of a spell to make oneself invisible:

> Athal Bathel nothe yhorum Asey elyungit gabellin semenei mecheno Bal habenentior mero meclab Halalerly Balnein Tigimiel pligas peneme Fruora Hean Ha Ararna Avira Ayla Ayes soye heremies surey levezo Haay Beruchata Acath turab Buchare Caralin per misericordiam habebit et go mortales perficiat hoc corpus ut invisibiliter ire passim.

Invisibility spells are commonly given in the grimoires. Aleister Crowley claimed to have used one to escape successfully from a murderous mob in Calcutta.

Another name that should be mentioned here is that of Honorius of Thebes, supposed author of a book in the Solomonic tradition referred to by medieval authors as the *Liber Sacratus*, the *Liber Juratus* or the *Sworn Book of Honorius*. The fourteenth-century Latin manuscripts of this text, one of which belonged to the playwright Ben Johnson, contain a preface describing the origin of the book. According to this account, the Pope and his cardinals had passed a decree aiming at the complete abolition of the magic art and condemning magicians to death. The grounds for this were that magicians and necromancers were injuring everyone, transgressing the statutes of the Church, invoking demons and bringing ignorant people to damnation by their tricks. These charges the magicians hotly denied, saying that the accusations were inspired by the Devil, who wished to keep a monopoly of such marvels. The magicians declared that it was impossible for a wicked or impure man to work truly by the magic art. They also claimed to have been forewarned by their art of the legislation against them, but they had hesitated to summon demons to their aid lest those spirits use the opportunity to destroy the populace utterly. Instead, an assembly of eighty-nine masters of the art of magic, from Naples, Athens and Toledo, had chosen Honorius, son of Euclid, a master of Thebes, to reduce their magic books to one volume containing ninety-three chapters, which could be more readily concealed and preserved. Each new recipient of the book was required to swear an oath that he would never give it to anyone else until he was on his death-bed, and furthermore that he would never give it to a woman or to anyone who was not of mature years and proven fidelity. Hence the name *Sworn Book*.

Thorndike describes the book as follows:

> The text is full of the names of spirits, prayers in strange words, supposedly derived from Hebrew or Chaldaic, and other gibberish. Series of letters and figures often occur and names inscribed in stars, hexagons and circles. An English translation in a fifteenth-century manuscript is adorned with pictures of rows of spirits dressed like monks in robes and caps but with angelic wings. The text does not seem to be complete in any of the manuscripts I have examined, but Sloane 3854 of the fourteenth century contains an apparently complete table of contents ...[5]

According to this contents list, the book is a comprehensive manual of the magic art. Subjects dealt with include: the great name of God containing seventy-two letters, the angels found in the different spheres of heaven and at the four points of the compass, their names, powers, seals and virtues, the characteristics of the stars and planets and the nature of their influences, the various demons and the means of controlling them, and methods of bringing about changes in the weather.

The *Sworn Book of Honorius* appears to have played a key role in medieval magic. It was clearly what might be called a 'seed work'. Probably used as a standard manual of magic among small groups of occultists and by individual magicians, it would have been copied out again and again and disseminated throughout Europe.

The name Honorius is also that of four popes, and to one of them is ascribed one of the most notorious grimoires of all time, the *Grimoire of Pope Honorius the Great*. Eliphas Lévi, in his *History of Magic*, speculates that its author was one Cadalus, Bishop of Parma, who in the eleventh century vainly attempted to seize the papal throne and called himself Honorius II. It seems to me much more likely, however, that the attribution is a result of a confusion with Honorius of Thebes and the *Sworn Book* — one of the many confusions that are found in the history of grimoires. Lévi claims that the *Grimoire of Honorius* played a part in the assassination of the Archbishop of Paris on 3 January 1857 at the church of Saint-Etienne du Mont. Soon after the event Lévi saw a sketch of the assassin and recognized him as a young priest who had called on him a year earlier asking how he could obtain a copy of the *Grimoire of Honorius*, explaining that he was 'seeking the realization of a thought' and had 'something to do'. As the young man was leaving he had turned to Lévi and said: 'Before long you will hear something ... you will hear me spoken of.' Lévi concluded that the priest had found the grimoire, carried out its instructions for evocation and 'prepared himself for the murder by a series of sacrileges'.[6]

The black reputation of the *Grimoire of Honorius* no doubt rests partly on the way in which it shamelessly exploits the name of the Pope and attempts to give a Christian colouring to the often barbaric-sounding rituals in it. The book begins with what purports to be a papal bull in which the pseudo-Pope confers on the brethren of the Church the authority to invoke and command spirits — an authority that had hitherto been vested only in the Pope himself. The fact that the book was a blatant forgery helped to give it a *succès de scandale*, but when one examines the contents one finds that they are mostly fairly innocuous, apart from one ritual which involves killing a black cock and removing its eyes, tongue and heart which are then dried in the rays of the sun and reduced to powder. This and other procedures, from a printed version of the grimoire published at Rome in 1760, will be found quoted extensively in Idries Shah's *The Secret Lore of Magic*.

As in the case of Solomon, the pseudo-Honorius has many imitators, so that it is difficult to identify the original grimoire. I examined two versions in the Bibliothèque Nationale in Paris (bound together in manuscript 24245). These contain separate lists of demons. Here, for example, are some of those listed in the first manuscript.

> Sates. Appears as a girl, confers invisibility and instructs in the virtues of herbs.
> Levins. As a fly. Gives gold, money and houses. He may only be summoned once.
> Neron. As a bird. Instructs in the curing of ills, brings glory to armies.
> Naymon. Occidental. As a crowned woman riding on a dromedary.
> He teaches the hidden sciences ...

The first printed version of *Honorius* appeared in 1629, and thereafter imitations continued to be published as late as the nineteenth century. During the course of this investigation we shall find other groups of grimoires in which a famous name has gathered around it a mass of bogus material.

6.
Magic and the Church

The attitude of the Church towards magic was ambivalent, as can be seen right from the beginning of the Christian era. Although Augustine and the early Church fathers had condemned magical practices, it was in fact impossible for the Church to banish magic. All it could do was to try to keep dealings with the supernatural in the hands of the clergy. It could not, for example, deny that demons existed, for Christ Himself had cast them out. But it could attempt to reserve to itself the right to carry out exorcisms and forbid laymen to have any dealings with the demonic or spirit world. This prohibition, however, was difficult to enforce since many innocuous forms of demonic magic and spirit worship were practised widely as part of surviving folk traditions. Pope Innocent III, in the thirteenth century, grew apoplectic when he heard that the pagan inhabitants of the Baltic coast were worshipping the sun, the moon, the winds and the rivers when they should have been worshipping God; and he sent an army to convert them. But such practices persisted, and persist today, even in the most Christianized parts of Europe.

Other forms of magic presented an even greater problem for the Church. Astrology, for example, was widely accepted by churchmen as a perfectly legitimate art. The thirteenth-century astrologer and seer, Michael Scot, was also a respected clergyman and enjoyed the favour of two popes. Michael was a Lowland Scot who settled in Sicily as astrologer to the brilliant Hohenstaufen Emperor Frederick II, who had his court there. He translated the works of Aristotle for Frederick and also wrote a treatise on astrology. Although he condemns demonic magic, his work is full of magical information, such as the occult virtues of certain words, herbs and precious stones, and the conjurations appropriate to different hours of the day and night. Michael Scot became legendary as a magician, and in Sir Walter Scott's *Lay of the Last Minstrel* he is credited with having 'cleft the Eildon Hills in three and bridled the Tweed with a curb of stone'.

The example of Michael Scot shows how astrology and related arts could be tolerated by the medieval Church, although periodic attempts were made to check the practice of them. And if you accepted astrology it was difficult not to accept its magical implications, such as the picking of a herb at the appropriate astrological time. Alchemy, too, was a widely accepted science, and numerous monasteries throughout Europe are alleged to have had alchemical laboratories. But alchemy, again, involves magical correspondences, magical imagery and magical procedures. Medicine was another field where it was almost impossible to avoid magic. One of the most important early medieval medical treatises was the Anglo-Saxon *Leech-Book of Bald and Cild,* written in the tenth century, which contained a mixture of medical and magical lore culled from classical authors and from folk traditions. The remedies are often accompanied by spells in which Christian and pagan elements are mingled. The following, for example, is a recipe for 'a salve against the elfin race and nocturnal visitors, and for women with whom the devil hath carnal commerce':

> One takes the ewe hop plant, wormwood, bishopwort, lupin, ashthroat, henbane, harewort, viper's bugloss, heatherberry plants, cropleek, garlic, grains of hedgerife, githrife and fennel. These herbs are put in a vessel and placed beneath the altar where nine masses are sung over them. They are then boiled in butter and mutton fat; much holy salt is added; the salve is strained through a cloth; and what remains of the worts is thrown into running water. The patient's forehead and eyes are to be smeared with this ointment and he is further to be censed with incense and signed often with the sign of the cross.[1]

This kind of remedy would have come under the heading of 'natural magic', that is to say the kind of magic that is concerned with the wonders of the natural world and man's use of them. Natural magic would also include planetary correspondences and the properties of metals and precious stones. Two other main kinds of magic were also recognized in the Middle Ages: theurgy (the invocation of occult forces for elevating purposes) and demonic magic (the more sinister practices, such as necromancy and demonic conjuration). In fact, however, the distinction between these categories was very blurred.

The whole attitude of the Church towards magic was therefore riddled with inconsistencies and contradictions. We find widespread tolerance, even encouragement of certain forms of magic, and what is more we find these practised even by the clergy themselves. At the same time there was always the fear of overstepping the mark and arousing the Church's condemnation. Sometimes the Church would reach out and silence a troublesome individual writer. And when it felt its dogmas or power to be fundamentally threatened it would act with ruthless determination to eradicate the cause, although the methods it used were sometimes clumsy and often enabled its intended victims to escape.

Typical of these methods was the *Index Librorum Prohibitorum*, the Index of Forbidden Books or, more simply, the Index, which was an attempt to combat the spread of heresy in the form of the printed word. Before the establishment of the Index, books had of course frequently been banned as heretical by the Inquisition (established in 1233), but by the mid sixteenth century it was thought necessary to set up a special system of censorship. The invention of printing in the mid fifteenth century had placed a new weapon in the hands of potentially subversive writers, yet it took a hundred years before the Church became sufficiently alarmed to issue its first list of prohibited books, which was published under the auspices of the Inquisition in 1557. In 1571, Pope Pius V established a special Congregation of the Index to supervise the list and amend it when necessary. The Congregation continued until 1917, when its function was incorporated into the Holy Office. The Index was finally abolished in 1966, by which time it had been revised more than forty times, with titles being added and deleted. Apart from the books that were totally banned, there was another category that had to be submitted for certain dangerous passages to be excised.

The Index was enforced with varying degrees of severity in different countries. A version issued at Lisbon in 1624 was preceded by an edict stating that all books on the Index were to be handed over to the Inquisition. Whoever after thirty days still possessed any heretical books would be liable to excommunication and could be prosecuted as an enemy of the faith. Furthermore, anyone who failed to denounce a person possessing such books was also considered to have committed an offence.

Magical books were, predictably, one of the main categories of literature to be found on the list. An Index issued at Parma in 1580 included names of Arnald de Villanova, Jerome Cardan, Raymond Lull, Paracelsus and Cornelius Agrippa.[2] In the seventeenth century many more such prohibitions were issued. In 1609, for example, the *Steganographia* of Trithemius was placed on the list (a work to which we shall return in detail). But the clumsiness of the Index as a weapon of censorship is shown by the fact that many books were not entered on it until many years after their publication. For instance, Strozzi Cigogna's *Palazzio degl'incanti* (Palace of Incantations), dealing with good and bad spirits, goetic magic and so on, was not placed on the Index until eighteen years after its publication at Vicenza in 1605, by which time it had been translated into German and Latin. The omissions from the list are equally striking and paradoxical. One work that escaped being forbidden was Torreblanca Villapando's *Daemonologia* (first published in 1618), an edition of which was dedicated to the Bishop of Würzburg. In Spain it was expurgated in three places, but never placed on the Index. In the eighteenth century the number of prohibitions fell, but one notable victim was the *Comte de Gabalis* by the Abbé de Villars (1670), which was put on the Index in 1712.

It must have been particularly irritating to the administrators of the Inquisition to discover numerous grimoires that were allegedly compiled as manuals of exorcism for the exclusive use of the clergy. One of these was published at Cologne in 1804 under the title of *Conclavis Romanis*, with an introduction by Johann Anton Schmidt 'of the Society of Jesus'. Whether or not Schmidt was a genuine Jesuit, his introduction makes interesting reading:

> Never before have the secret magical writings that this book contains been published, and should still not be. They were the property of the monasteries, which preserved them as incalculably valuable possessions. It was only very seldom and by peculiar chance, or sometimes through the payment of large sums of money, that such a manuscript came into private hands. They contain the high science of dealing with supernatural beings and calling forth good as well as bad spirits in a godly manner for various services through the use of successful prayers, powerful quotations and effective means of coercion ... This art ... has degenerated into evil misuse and has been abused in a repugnant manner. Some people have even given themselves freely as slaves to evil spirits by entering into impious pacts. Hence this godless purpose and abhorrent misuse has been rightly forbidden by both Church and secular authorities, and all writings of this nature have been carefully sought out and collected. It is also known that His Holiness Pope Pius VI in the year 1782 during his discussion with Kaiser Joseph II ... declared a ban against such works. For these reasons very few original magical books can be found, and it was only with the greatest trouble that it was possible to gather together these works ... in which the true science of the spirits is contained.[3]

The *Conclavis Romanis* is prefixed with a papal dispensation allowing the summoning of spirits with a grimoire, provided that the appropriate prayers and benedictions are recited over the grimoire before the operation. If this is not done, it is stated, the ritual will be ineffective. Most likely the whole book is a fraud, but such frauds are an important part of this story.

7.
DOCTOR UNIVERSALIS

The history of grimoires abounds in paradoxes, and one of the strangest is the fact that a revered theologian and saint of the Roman Catholic Church should also be renowned as a sorcerer and author of magical textbooks. He is known to posterity as Albertus Magnus (1193–1280). In his day he was widely regarded as the most learned man in Europe and was dubbed 'Doctor Universalis' on account of his wide knowledge. Born into an aristocratic Swabian family, he bore the title Count of Bollstadt. Possessed of a desire to study natural sciences, he travelled to Italy and enrolled at the University of Padua. Here, at the age of thirty-seven, he joined the Dominican order whose founder, Saint Dominic, had died seven years earlier. The Dominicans were teachers of the faith, stern upholders of the purity of Church doctrine and administrators of the Inquisition. So it is curious that one of their greatest members should have been famous as a practitioner of forbidden arts, even if this reputation is legendary.

At first Albert showed little promise as a scholar. Then one night he dreamed that the Virgin Mary endowed him with intellectual powers. After that his progress was spectacular. Having completed his theological studies at Cologne he travelled around Europe teaching at various Dominican centres. Then he spent three years at the University of Paris, where his lectures were attended by such large numbers that he had to hold them in the open air.

Subsequently he returned to Cologne where one of his pupils was Thomas Aquinas who was to carry on Albert's work of incorporating the teachings of Aristotle into Christian doctrine. Between them they had an incalculable effect on medieval Christianity. Another of Albert's pupils at Cologne was Ulrich Engelbert of Strasbourg, who later became head of the Dominican order and constructed the Cathedral organ at Strasbourg by means of technical knowledge imparted to him by Albert.

There followed more travels, then a period as Archbishop of Regensburg, where Albert occupied the castle of Stauff on a height overlooking the Danube. Rumours began to circulate about the curious scientific experiments which he carried on there, and the atmosphere became so hostile towards him that he felt obliged to leave. Relieved, at his own request, of his bishopric and of his vows of obedience and poverty, Albert nevertheless remained in the order and for the rest of his life continued to travel and to play an active role in the Church. He died at Cologne at 1280. Six and a half centuries later, in 1931, he was canonized.

Albert left behind a colossal corpus of written work covering every branch of contemporary knowledge apart from law. 'Albert', it was said, 'was great in magic, greater in philosophy and supreme in theology.' But it is his magical reputation that concerns us here. This rests largely on two magical works that bear his name, one partly genuine, the other falsely attributed to him.

The first is the *Book of Secrets of Albert the Great,* often called the *Great Albert,*[1] a compilation of various writings, some of which were extracted from Albertus's works after his death and put together by an unknown editor with other miscellaneous writings such as a treatise by Michael Scot. It contains a work called *de Secretis Mulierum* (of the Secrets of Women) dealing with conception and pregnancy. Other sections give information on the characteristics of precious stones, the influences of the planets, the properties of substances and how to make use of them for practical purposes and the curing of certain maladies. Part of the *Great Albert* is quoted in Part II of this book.

The *Great Albert* began to circulate in manuscript during the first half of the fourteenth century and, thanks to the legendary reputation of its author, came to be widely in demand. The original text was in Latin, but it was soon translated into Italian, German, French and English. After the invention of printing in the middle of the fifteenth century the book appeared in numerous editions: in 1477 it was published at Venice, in 1480 at Lyons, in 1489 at Passau, in 1500 at Paris. In 1550 an edition was published at Lyons by the Beringos Brothers (who also published Cornelius Agrippa's *de Occulta Philosophia*) to be followed by many subsequent editions until 1604, when *de Secretis Mulierum* was placed on the Index of Forbidden Books. Henceforth, for the next century or so, this part of the work, and often the whole grimoire, appeared entirely in Latin. But a French edition of the work excluding the *de Secretis Mulierum* was published in the seventeenth century by Jacques Oudot, a well-known publisher of popular works. After 1760 vernacular editions of the book began to appear again, and have continued to do so up to the present day.

A book of secrets can be defined as a proto-scientific handbook of recipes and information, and the material in the *Great Albert* lies mostly on the borderline between magic and science. It contains no instructions for the evocation of demons, but the information given on such matters as herbs and precious stones is based on a set of assumptions which we would now call magical, such as the notion that each herb is governed by a particular planet. The section entitled *A Treatise on the Wonders of the World* is written in a tone of scientific observation but contains much magical material. For example, Albertus quotes an ancient recipe whereby 'if a man finds that his wife scorns his attentions he should take the fat of a he-goat, neither too large nor too small. After he has rubbed his penis with this material and made love to her he can be sure that she will scorn others and love only him.'

If the *Great Albert* is half way between magic and science, the *Little Albert* is more unashamedly magical. This contains no material written by Albert himself but is a compendium from the works of other writers, chiefly the *De Subtilitate* by Jerome Cardan (1501-1576) and the *Natural Magic* of Giambattista della Porta (1540-1615). Cardan was an Italian polymath and one of the leading figures in Renaissance learning. He wrote numerous treatises on subjects ranging from mathematics to medicine, and like many Renaissance intellectuals his outlook was greatly influenced by Hermetic ideas. Della Porta was also a many-faceted man. His *Natural Magic,* which is quoted in the second part of this book, became one of the most widely read works of its kind.

There is also an alchemical section in the *Little Albert* which is taken from a treatise entitled *Letter from a Philosopher on the Secret of the Great Work* by Alexandre Limojon de Saint-Didier (1630–1689), who, besides being an alchemist, was a diplomat who undertook confidential missions for Louis XIV. The *Little Albert* also contains a small section on talismans and their value.

The whole book is a confusing hotch-potch. Nevertheless, like the *Great Albert,* with which it has often appeared in the same volume, it sold extremely well from the time of its first publication in the early eighteenth century.

8.

The Strange Case of Nicolas Flamel and the Book of Abraham the Jew

Occasionally in the annals of occult literature we hear of some book that has appeared at a critical time and place, played an important role and then vanished into the realms of legend. Such a book features in the remarkable story of the French alchemist Nicolas Flamel, a figure whose life is surrounded by an aura of mystery.

The outer facts of Flamel's life are briefly as follows. He was born in about 1330 and died in 1417. He lived in Paris in the rue des Ecrivains in the shadow of the church of St. Jacques de la Boucherie, whose curiously haunting tower is all that remains of the building. He was a man of simple piety who lived a quiet and retiring life. While earning his living as a bookseller, scribe and legal draftsman, he devoted his real energies to the study and practice of alchemy.

Suddenly, after years of unrewarding toil, assisted by his devoted wife Pernelle, Flamel apparently became rich. He established an alms house in the rue de Montmorency, built a portico for the church of St. Jacques and erected two arcades in the nearby Cemetery of the Innocents which he decorated with alchemical allegories. His own manner of living, however, remained simple and modest.

What was the source of his fortune? The answer seems to be that Flamel finally discovered the secret of transmutation thanks to a mysterious grimoire which an unknown man brought into his shop one day. A description of this volume appears in Flamel's book *Le Livre des figures hieroglyphiques de Nicolas Flamel* (published in 1682):

There fell into my hands, for the sum of two florins, a gilded book, very old and large. It was not of paper or parchment like all the others but was made of the delicate bark (as it seemed to me) of tender young trees. The cover was of copper, well bound, all engraved with letters or strange figures which, for my part, I believe could have been Greek characters or those of some other ancient language ... As for the contents, the bark leaves had been engraved, with admirable diligence using an iron point to write fair and neat Latin letters which had been coloured. It contained thrice seven leaves, for so were the leaves numbered at the top, and every seventh leaf contained no writing. Instead on the first seventh leaf was painted a Virgin with serpents swallowing her up; on the second was shown a cross whereon a serpent was crucified; and on the last were depicted deserts or wildernesses, in the midst of which ran many fair fountains from whence there issued a number of serpents running up and down, here and there. Upon the first of the leaves was written in great capital letters of gold: ABRAHAM THE JEW, PRINCE, PRIEST, LEVITE, ASTROLOGER, AND PHILOSOPHER, TO THE NATION OF THE JEWS, BY THE WRATH OF GOD DISPERSED AMONG THE GAULES, SENDETH HEALTH.

After this it was filled with great execrations and curses (with the word Maranatha being often repeated) against any person that should cast his eyes upon it unless he were a sacrificer or scribe. The man who sold me this book did not know what it was worth, any more than I when I bought it. I believe it had been stolen or taken by violence from the Jews, or found hidden in some part of their ancient habitation. Within the book, on the second page, he [the author] comforted his nation, counselling them to eschew vices and above all idolatry, attending with sweet patience the coming of the Messiah, who should vanquish all the kings of the earth and should reign with his people in glorie eternally ... in the third page, and in all the other writings that followed, to help his captive nation to pay their tributes to the Roman Emperors, and to do other things which I will not speak of, he taught them in common words the transmutation of metals; he painted the vessels by the sides and he informed them of the colours and of all the rest, except the First Agent, of which he said not a word, except that (as he said) on the fourth and fifth pages he had painted it with very great cunning and workmanship, for, though it was well and

> intelligently depicted, no man could ever have been able to understand it without being well versed in their Cabala ...[1]

Flamel and his wife studied this book for twenty years without success, then Flamel in desperation set out for Spain, ostensibly on a pilgrimage to Saint James of Compostella but in fact to see if he could find a Jew who would be able to explain the grimoire to him. Whether or not he found the Jew, soon after his return to Paris his efforts were finally crowned with success, as he himself recorded: 'At last I found what I desired. It was on 17th January at about midday at my house, with only Pernelle present, in the year 1382.' Flamel goes on to say that on 25 April, using the 'red stone' and mercury, he succeeded with the aid of Pernelle in producing a quantity of pure gold.

We do not know what happened to the book that Flamel possessed, but like most grimoires of that era it was probably one of a family of manuscripts, each being a copy or version of some 'parent' text. In the Bibliothèque Nationale in Paris is a manuscript (number FR 14765) that might have belonged to the same family. This is entitled *Figures hiéroglyphiques d'Habraham Juif* Hieroglyphic Figures of Abraham the Jew) and consists largely of alchemical formulae, beautifully illustrated with coloured drawings, one of which illustrates a crucified serpent. This and the name 'Abraham the Jew' in the title form two points of similarity with Flamel's book. Its date of composition was not recorded, but it had at one time belonged to a certain Chevalier Molinier who had lived in the time of Louis XIV.

One of the striking things about this Bibliothèque Nationale manuscript is the exalted tone in which it is written, quite unlike the debased flavour of so many of the grimoires. In fact, the alchemical texts as a whole belong to an altogether higher category than most of the grimoires dealing with purely demonic magic.

One of the injunctions given in this text is never to act 'against the Sovereign Creator, your own good or that of your brother'. The aim of the magician is to research into the secrets of nature. 'Natural magic', the writer states, 'has greatly degenerated during the last few centuries to the point where its name is as despised now as it was once honoured, just as the names "tyrant" and "sophist", which were once highly esteemed, have come to be held in abhorrence.' The author goes on to trace the venerable history of magic, from the Egyptians, Babylonians and Chaldeans, via King Solomon, Apollonius of Tyana, Pythagoras, Socrates and the Three Magi of the New Testament.

Another manuscript that possibly belongs to the same family is *The Book of the Sacred Magic of Abra-Melin the Mage, as delivered by Abraham the Jew unto his son Lamech,* AD *1458,* made famous by S.L. MacGregor Mathers, founder of the Golden Dawn, who translated it from a manuscript in the Arsenal Library in Paris. Although the date of composition is after Flamel's death, the text might have been based on the book that Flamel used. We shall return to the subject of the Abra-Melin book when it reappears in the nineteenth century as an inspiration to Aleister Crowley and others. Meanwhile we must leave the thread of high magic and the alchemical tradition and take up again the thread of demonic magic.

9.
THE FAUST LEGEND

In the whole history and mythology of magic one name stands out above all others as embodying its romance, terror and sinister fascination: the name of Doctor Faust (of Faustus). In the famous plays about him, written by Marlowe and Goethe, he is depicted as a scholar, frustrated by the limitations of academic study, who turns to sorcery and makes a pact with the Devil. A wonderfully atmospheric painting by Delacroix shows him in his study confronting the figure of Mephistopheles who has just appeared. They face each other across a table on which is propped up a vast grimoire which Faust has been using. In Goethe's play two grimoires feature. The first is mentioned when Faust, full of disgust at the barrenness of scholarship, takes down a book by Nostradamus, with the words:

> Up and away! A distant land
> Awaits me in this secret book
> From Nostradamus' very hand,
> Nor for a better guide I look.[1]

Leafing through the book he lights upon the 'sign of the Macrocosm' (normally depicted as a six-pointed Star of David). This scene has been represented in a well-known etching by Rembrandt, in which Faust looks up to see the sign shining through the window of his room.

Looking further through the book, he comes upon the sign of the Spirit of the Earth and declares:

> A curious change affects me in this sign:
> You, kindred sprite of Earth,
> Come strangely nearer;

My spirits rise, my powers are stronger, clearer,
As from the glow of a refreshing wine.

He seizes the book and calls upon the spirit, whereupon a reddish flame shoots up, and the elemental appears in the flame. Faust proclaims himself to be the spirit's equal, but the latter vanishes after scorning him with the words:

You match the spirit that you comprehend,
Not me.

Having been rejected by the Earth Spirit, he aspires to reach beyond the veil by taking poison, but in a later scene he is followed into the house by a black poodle which assumes gigantic size. Realizing it to be a supernatural being, Faust reaches for a second grimoire with the words:

For such a hybrid brood of hell,
The Key of Solomon will serve me well.

Goethe evidently knew the Solomonic literature well, for he was familiar with the doctrine of the four groups of elemental spirits which plays such an important role in magic. With the book in his hand, Faust continues:

First, to confront this thing of hell,
I must repeat the four-fold spell:
Salamander bright shall burn,
Sylph invisible shall turn,
Undine flow within her wave,
Kobold [ie gnome] shall slave.

The dog remains unaffected until Faust holds up to him the sign of the cross. This frightens him into showing himself as Mephistopheles, dressed in the garb of a wandering scholar. Thus begins the association between Faust and Mephistopheles.

Apart from the Faust plays by Marlowe and Goethe and the pictures by Delacroix and Rembrandt, there are many other works of art featuring the notorious magician. There is an opera on the subject by Gounod, an oratorio by Berlioz, and a symphony by Franz Liszt. There have also been films, the most famous of which was the German one made in 1960 with Gustav Gründgens as Mephistopheles and Will Quadflieg as Faust. There is also a French version with Gérard Philippe as Faust, and an Anglo-American production of Marlowe's play with Richard Burton in the title role.

Behind such fictitious portrayals lies a real historical figure who, like King Arthur, has become overlaid with the accretions of myth. In Goethe's play he is called Heinrich. In reality his name was Johann Georg Faust (from the Latin *faustus* meaning lucky or 'auspicious'), and he was born at Knittlingen in Württemberg in about 1480, possibly the illegitimate son of a servant girl and her employer. There is no record of his education at school or university, and his title of 'doctor' was probably adopted by himself. In the early part of the sixteenth century he became a familiar figure in market-places and inns throughout Germany as a wonder-worker who boasted of his vast knowledge and his power over the spirits. The story of the pact with Mephistopheles was undoubtedly added later by folklore, for the object of magic was to control demons, not to sell them your soul.

It is difficult to extract concrete facts about his life, though there are many vague reports of his activities. He is supposed to have cast a horoscope for the Prince-Archbishop of Bamberg and to have persuaded the Abbott of Maulbronn to set up an alchemical laboratory for him so that he could save the Abbot from bankruptcy. His fellow occultists seem to have regarded him with distrust and dislike. Trithemius, Abbot of Sponheim, for example, condemned him as a cheat and a homosexual. The accusation of homosexuality was also the reason for his being banned from entering Nuremberg in 1532. In his sixties he is supposed to have met his end in a laboratory accident.

Contemporary records of the historical Faust cease in about 1540, and soon afterwards the legendary Faust makes his appearance. The earliest extant collection of stories about him appears in the notebook of a Nuremberg teacher called Christoph Rossbirt, written in about 1570. This was followed by the so-called Wolfenbüttel manuscript of between 1572 and 1587 (a printed version was published at Wolfenbüttel in 1892 under the title *Historia D. Johannis Fausti des Zauberers nach der*

Wolfenbütteler Handschrift, edited by Gustav Milchsack).

The first printed book about Faust was the *Spies Faustbuch*, published by Johann Spies at Frankfurt-am-Main in 1587. This proved a great popular success and was soon pirated by other publishers in various parts of Germany. Then came extended and more elaborate accounts of Faust's career, such as the *Faustbuch* produced by Georg Widmann and published at Hamburg in 1599. After a cooling of interest in the Faust material during the Thirty Years' War (1618–48) and its aftermath, a revised version of Widman's book appeared at Nuremberg in 1674, edited by Nicolaus Pfitzer. The last German book belonging to this phase was the *Faustbuch des Christlich Meynenden*, essentially a condensation of Widman, first published in the early 1700s and subsequently reprinted many times. Translations of these books were published in many countries outside Germany, including England, Holland and France. The English Faust Book, on which Marlowe's tragedy is based, was entitled *The Historie of the damnable life, and deserved death of Doctor John Faustus*. It was translated by one 'P.F.' and published in London in Elizabethan times, the earliest extant edition dating from 1592.

In addition to these legendary accounts of Faust's life, there began to proliferate books of magical formulae purporting to have been written by the notorious doctor himself. The most famous of these is the *Magia naturalis et innaturalis, oder dreifacher Höllenzwang* (Natural and unnatural magic, or threefold Harrowing of Hell). The term *Höllenzwang* (Harrowing of Hell) was to appear in the titles of many of the other pseudo-Faust grimoires. The *Magia naturalis et innaturalis*, published at Passau in 1505, is a hotch-potch of magical lore taken from the works of Agrippa and others. One of its amusing features is that it postulates a hierarchy of demons based on the hierarchy of the Holy Roman Empire, with Grand Dukes, Kings, Princes, Electors, Counts Palatine and so on down to the peasants. Different parts of the text conflict over the names of these demons, but the seven Electors are at one point listed as: Bludon, Marbuel, Ariel, Aciel, Barbiel, Mephistophiel and Apadiel.

These Electors are, according to E.M. Butler, based on the seven so-called *maskim* of the Akkadians (the people of Akkad in Mesopotamia, a civilization that flourished in the first and second millenia BC). The *maskim* were the inverse forms of the planetary deities. Another Elector, Aciel, who finds hidden treasure, is a version of Asiel (or Aziel), the Akkadian 'black sun', that is the inverse of the daylight sun. Aciel features as one of the most important demons in the Faust literature, arguably more important even than Mephistopheles, and very difficult to handle.

The inclusion of Ariel in the list is interesting in view of his reappearance in Shakespeare's *The Tempest*. The character of Ariel, as it emerges from the book, has much in common with the figure of Hermes or Mercury, and indeed his planet is given as Mercury. 'Like Hermes,' writes E.M. Butler, 'the messenger of the gods, he wanders widely over crags and dales; and like quicksilver he is difficult to constrain, hates to be tied and therefore dislikes pacts. Shakespeare's Ariel also fretted against the bonds which bound him to Prospero.'[2]

Thus we see here a tradition stretching from ancient Mesopotamia to the Shakespearean stage, via the grimoires.

Interestingly, the *Magia* gives a different picture from the legendary accounts of Faust's life. In the latter he is irrevocably doomed to damnation through his pact with Mephistopheles. The *Magia,* however, advises the magician that, if he wishes to make a pact with a hellish spirit he should leave the way open to renege on the agreement by continuing to attend mass, thereby keeping himself in good odour with God for when the time came to renounce the pact. Furthermore the Faust of the *Magia* gives the impression that he is master of the spirits, handling them as a lion-tamer might handle his charges. One Faustian grimoire, however, *The Black Raven,* contains a unilateral pact with Lucifer. As for the actual ceremonies described in the Faustian grimoires, E.M. Butler points out that they lack the pomp and grandeur of the Solomonic rites.

The *Magia* and *The Black Raven* were only two of many magical textbooks attributed to Faust. The others included a curious series of volumes purporting to have been issued under the auspices of the Vatican in order to give them a veneer of respectability. Other manuals, both Faustian and non-Faustian, were ascribed to the Jesuits. One, for example, *Doctor Fausts grosser und gewaltiger Höllenzwang* (Doctor Faust's Great and powerful Harrowing of Hell) bore the imprint of a Jesuit college in Prague and the date 1509, twenty-five years before the founding of the Jesuit order.

The authors of the bogus Faust manuals resorted to other devices to give them appeal. One of them decided to create a grimoire with a maritime flavour entitled *Doctor Faustus's grosser und gewaltiger Meergeist* (Doctor Faust's Great and Powerful Sea Spirit), published at Amsterdam in 1692. This dangled the familiar prospect of treasure before the reader and exploited the fascination which sea monsters exert on the imagination. Here is a passage from the grimoire:

> ... Forneus, who will appear as a sea monster, Vepar, like a siren, and Zaleus, like a crocodile. They will all come teeming forth surrounded by many millions of spirits in monstrous shapes, black, with snakes for hair and tongues of fire, terrifying to behold. One can now demand of Lucifer as much gold and silver and jewels or any other useful treasure which lies in the sea, grows in the sea or has been cast into the depths of the sea by shipwreck, as one likes. He will immediately command his sea-spirits to go and fetch it. They now with all their black attendant spirits pass through the ocean and all the waters of the earth, and one spirit alone, Paymon, remains behind to attend Lucifer. What a roaring on the sea or in the waters; what a thundering and lightning in the air; and what a howling and wailing among the sea-monsters and the creatures in the waters will then be heard! For these also tremble at the obedience of the hellish spirits who rush with lightning speed to perform their master's orders. The whole journey takes three minutes.[3]

Although one reacts with amusement to the passage one can only reflect that it illustrates the sad debasement to which the great magical tradition of the Akkadian-Chaldean inscriptions and the Graeco-Egyptian papyri had descended. Many more debasements were to occur before the tradition was to be reformed and given back a measure of its ancient dignity.

10.
The Golden Age of Magic

In the Middle Ages magical works of all kinds were regarded as objects to be avoided by right-thinking Christians. It is true that some churchmen practised magic and a few were even bold enough to write openly about it, but generally magic was surrounded by taboos, and magical works were documents to be read in secret. Then came the Renaissance. Religious inhibitions were weakened, and the light of human enquiry shone into many dark corners. What happened when this light fell on the old magical texts?

One of the first things that the Renaissance occult scholars discovered was that magic could be a lofty spiritual discipline as well as a means of evoking demons for base purposes. This was, for example, the view of Marsilio Ficino (1433–1499), who translated the Hermetic writings for his patron Cosimo de Medici, ruler of Florence and one of the great moving spirits of Renaissance Italy. One of the Hermetic treatises which Ficino translated was the *Asclepius* which describes the drawing down of divine forces into images by means of sympathetic magic, a practice of which Ficino himself approved. Frances Yates believes that the rehabilitation of the *Asclepius* by Ficino was 'one of the chief factors in the Renaissance revival of magic'.[1]

One of the ways in which Ficino practised his magical ideas was by singing 'Orphic songs'. It will be remembered from Chapter 5 that Orpheus, like Hermes, was regarded as one of the great sages of antiquity. The Orphic songs were incantations designed to attract favourable planetary influences. Ficino was in the habit of singing these songs accompanying himself on a lyre and using a simple melodic music which he believed to echo the 'music of the spheres' which Pythagoras had described.

This musical magic of the Orphic incantations had its visual counterpart in talismanic magic where the magicians contemplated objects or pictures that were imbued with the planetary virtues. This practice is believed to have had a strong influence on Renaissance art. Frances Yates believes, for example, that Botticelli's *Primavera* is really a complex talisman designed to transmit good planetary influences by depicting figures and images that have the appropriate planetary correspondences.

It is interesting that a Latin translation of the Arabic magical treatise, the *Picatrix*, also circulated widely among Renaissance scholars, and Frances Yates suggests that 'it may have been one of Ficino's authorities on talismans and sympathetic magic'.[2] Its influence can also be seen in the palace at Ferrara where the Duke of Borso d'Este decorated a room with paintings of the signs of the Zodiac and their sub-divisions, the thirty-six decans, a concept taken from Egyptian cosmology and incorporated into the astrological tradition. The images of the decans at Ferrara closely resemble the descriptions of them given in the *Picatrix*. The three decans of Aries, for example, are: 'a huge dark man with red eyes, holding a sword and clad in a white garment', 'a woman clad in green and lacking one leg' and 'a man holding a golden sphere and dressed in red'.[3] It seems likely that whoever painted these murals was familiar with the *Picatrix* and its decan figures, the Egyptian gods of time which Augustine had banned.

The Renaissance scholars who revived interest in magic approached the subject with varying attitudes. Ficino was at pains to point out to those who criticized his defence of magic that there were two kinds of magic: one demonic and wicked, the other natural and good. The latter, he affirmed, was the only kind he had practised or advocated.

A similar stance was taken up by another important esoteric scholar of Renaissance Italy, namely Pico della Mirandola (1463–1494). Whereas Ficino's field was the Hermetic writings, Pico's was the Qabalah. Frances Yates writes:

> This was a spiritual magic ... in the sense that it attempted to tap the higher spiritual powers, beyond the natural powers of the cosmos. Practical Cabala invokes angels, archangels, the ten sephiroth which are names or powers of God, God himself, by means some of which are similar to other magical procedures but more particularly through the power of the sacred Hebrew language. It is thus a much more ambitious kind of magic than Ficino's natural magic, and one which it would be impossible to keep apart from religion.[4]

At the age of twenty-four Pico went to Rome, taking with him nine hundred theses which he offered to defend in public debate. Many of these theses concerned magic, both the natural magic of Ficino and Cabalistic magic. The theses aroused the unfavourable attention of Pope Innocent VIII, infamous for the launching of the great witchcraft persecution. A commission was appointed to examine the theses, and thirteen of them were declared heretical or erroneous. Pico replied with an *Apologia* published in 1487, defending the rejected theses. Hounded by the Inquisition, Pico fled to France where he was arrested by Papal nuncios and imprisoned at Vincennes. He was released and allowed to return to Florence but did not obtain papal forgiveness and safety from the Inquisition until a year before his death at the age of thirty.

Pico wrote with approval of Ficino's Orphic incantations and other forms of what he called 'natural magic'. But Pico believed that natural magic on its own was a rather feeble instrument. In order to be effective it had to be combined with Cabala. It was all very well to draw down celestial influences through talismans and songs, but the Cabala enabled the magician to rise up in spirit through the spheres by contemplation of the Sephiroth.

Here was a magic totally different in spirit from the demonic formulae of the more debased medieval grimoires. And along with this change in the character of magic went a change in the status of the magician himself. The image of the cobwebbed medieval necromancer never entirely disappeared, but it bore little relation to men such as Ficino and Pico.

These Italian magicians and esoteric scholars had their counterparts all over Europe at this time, and one of the most significant was a German Benedictine named Johannes Trithemius (1462–1516) who is best known for his remarkable work, the *Steganographia*, a sort of combined grimoire and cipher manual which was to have a tremendous influence in the development of occult writings. In the introduction to his 1982 edition of part of this work, Adam McLean writes:

> Johannes Trithemius was perhaps the central figure in the evolution of the Western Esoteric tradition. He transformed the magic of the medieval period, synthesising it into a Renaissance Esoteric Art and Science, and the formative influence of his ideas spread all over Europe.[5]

Born at Trittenheim, near Trier on the Mosel into a poor family, Trithemius showed a remarkable early aptitude for learning and was guided by a mysterious mentor who appeared to him at Heidelberg and instructed him in the secret sciences. This mentor told him that on his journey back to Trittenheim he would find the key to his life. As it turned out, snow forced him to take shelter in the monastery at Sponheim near Bingen in the district of the Upper Rhine. Here he decided to settle, and at the age of twenty-three he became Abbot.

Under his aegis the monastery became a great centre of learning, and the library swelled to two thousand volumes, making it one of the biggest in Europe at that time. Adam McLean writes:

> This library, together with his scholarship and creative energy, gave Trithemius a degree of fame. People came from France, Italy and Germany to see this collection and to meet the great scholar. Princes and Kings, even the Emperor Maximilian I, sent emissaries to ask the advice of the Abbot of Sponheim ... Outwardly an Abbot of the Benedictine Order, Trithemius, however, was also an adept, an esoteric teacher, and he sought to inculcate a knowledge of the vast body of wisdom in the Western Occult Tradition. He sought the spiritual within this tradition to refashion it into a form suitable for the age ... As befits one who wished to work secretly, Trithemius was much pre-occupied with codes and magical alphabets, as is evidenced by his 'Steganographia' and 'Polygraphia', and it is likely that there is much encoded in his more respectable published material, for example in his Sermons and Prayers.[6]

The *Steganographia* is one of the most extraordinary books ever written, and must be taken on at least two levels. Superficially it is a grimoire for the conjuration of angels and spirits, with long, barbarous-sounding incantations. On another level it is a highly complex cipher manual with the instructions for encipherment contained in the incantations. Trithemius was not the first person to realize the usefulness of codes and ciphers, but he faced the same problem that all cryptographers have faced: namely how to devise a code or cipher that is comprehensible to your friends but cannot be cracked by your enemies. This problem becomes even more acute if you are actually writing a manual of cryptography, for how can you be sure tha it will be understood only by the worthy? Trithemius faces this problem in his preface, where he writes:

> I have considered it not the least part of my duty to prevent this important secret from reaching the ears of common, unskilled or wicked men, since it may instruct an untrained man to understand the mysteries. I have, therefore, cloaked it in secrecy, so that no one of those unskilled, no one except the most studious, might penetrate fully and completely to the heart of this knowledge and our meaning by his own ability, unless he receives from a teacher what the Hebrews call CABALA, of foremost importance in the most secret mysteries.[7]

Trithemius's system depends on a number of different modes of encipherment, each of which is named after a particular angel, and the instructions for using the ciphers are partly contained in conjurations that accompany the names. Chapter I, for example, describes a mode ruled over by the angel Pamersiel. When a message has been sent by this means, the recipient chants the following conjuration: 'Lamarton anoyr bulon madriel traschon ebrasothea panthenon nabrulges Camery itrasbier rubanthy nadres Calmosy ormenulan, ytules demy rabion hamorphyn.'[8] When this apparent gibberish is deciphered by taking every alternate letter of every alternate word it yields the message in a mixture of German and Latin: 'Nym die ersten bugstaben de omni verbo' (take the first letter of each word). But how does the recipient of the message know which mode is being used and thus which conjuration to recite? To find this out he also has to know that the sixteen angels governing the modes are linked with sixteen points of the compass, beginning with Pamersiel in the east, but Trithemius adds that 'the East is not where the sun rises on any day, but where it was originally created,which we call the Equinox.'[9] By this, Trithemius seems to mean that the east is to be equated with Aries, the traditional sign of the spring equinox. But how this is to be applied to the decipherment is not clear. There are also evidently other keys, not described in the book, which are necessary to operate the system fully.

All this raises the question why Trithemius should have used the form of a grimoire to convey his ciphering methods. To answer this we have to remember that Trithemius was operating in the tradition of the western mystery schools, such as the Rosicrucians, which were preserving a body of esoteric knowledge and preparing the way for the reform of mankind at a time when the tyranny of Church and state made it necessary for adherents of these schools to operate in secret. As Adam McLean writes:

> The myth of the 120 year entombment of Christian Rosencreutz in a sense refers to the long period of inner digestion and synthesis of esoteric traditions which was necessary for this new impulse to come about. We recognize this as stretching back to Trithemius, who at the end of the fifteenth century was gathering and synthesising the esoteric material that would later be woven into the fabric of Rosicrucianism. In this sense Trithemius has been called the first Rosicrucian.[10]

Trithemius's *Steganographia* can therefore be seen not as a work for the general public but a manual for his pupils and colleagues in the mystery school within which he worked. Apart from the neatness of having ciphers arranged in an angelic system and the suitability of barbarous conjurations for concealing instructions, the grimoire form had the advantage that by using it Trithemius would by implication be addressing himself to people who were in touch with magical currents of thought. A further advantage was that he could incorporate in the book deeper layers of teaching that were independent of the cipher system. Possibly Trithemius intended the conjurations in the book to be learned off-by-heart and used together with secret instructions that would only be transmitted by word of mouth from one initiate to another, thus ensuring that the initiates could communicate with one another in complete secrecy.

Among Trithemius's followers were two men who were to play an important role in carrying the occult tradition further: Agrippa and Paracelsus. Heinrich Cornelius Agrippa von Nettesheim was born at Cologne in 1486 and died at Grenoble in 1535. He led a wandering and insecure life as soldier, scholar and physician, travelling all over Europe and coming into contact with many of the leading minds of his day. He is most widely remembered for his three-volume work *Occult Philosophy (De Occulta Philosophia)*, which expounds magic in terms similar to Ficino and also shows the influence of the *Picatrix*. Long after writing this work, but before it was published, Agrippa changed his attitude and wrote a book, entitled *On the Vanity of Arts and Sciences*, in which he asserted that the only certain thing in the world was religious faith. Great confusion was caused in the public mind when the publication of this was followed by the delayed appearance of his three books of *Occult Philosophy*.

The first of these books deals with natural magic, that is magic operating in the elemental world. The second deals with celestial magic, and here Agrippa lists images symbolic of the signs, planets and decans. The image of Saturn, for example, is a man with a stag's head and camel's feet, seated on a throne, or a dragon, bearing a sickle in the right hand and an arrow in the left. And the decan images correspond roughly to those of the *Picatrix*. The third book is about ceremonial magic, and here he outlines a system of practical Qabalah. The underlying message of the whole work is that magic in its highest form is a religion whose priests worship the ultimate creator but understand the workings of all levels of creation and know how to manipulate them for the general good. Agrippa's book is therefore a step back towards the high magic of the ancient Egyptians that had become so debased over the centuries. One of the many people influenced by Agrippa's writings was Giordano Bruno who wished to revive the magical theocracy of Egypt and who died at the stake in Rome in 1600 after being condemned as a heretic by the Inquisition.

Before leaving the subject of Agrippa, it is necessary to mention the so-called *Fourth Book of Occult Philosophy* which appeared thirty years after Agrippa's death and is unquestionably spurious. Whereas the three earlier books are works of magical philosophy, the *Fourth Book* is a full-blooded grimoire. It takes its theoretical basis from the first three books, but then launches into detailed instructions for magical work. The pseudo-Agrippa illustrates the sigils of good and evil spirits, explains how to make pentacles, gives details of instruments and magical paraphernalia and instructs the reader in the carrying out of ceremonies. Even though spurious, this *Fourth Book of Occult Philosophy* had as great an influence in certain circles as the other three. A seventeenth-century English translation by Robert Turner was published together with a number of other grimoires such as the *Heptameron* of Peter de Abano.[11]

An important idea, which possibly originates from the *Fourth Book of Occult Philosophy* is that of the *Liber Spiritum (Book of the Spirits)*. The following passage from the *Fourth Book* describes this grimoire.

> Those magicians who make use of the assistance of demons in their operations have a special way of invoking them. They possess a book called the *Book of the Spirits*, which is also consecrated, and in which the names of the spirits are written, who must then swear an oath to be obedient to the magician in this world. The paper of this book must be made of virgin paper which has never been used before. On the left side of the book is seen the image of the spirit, on the right side his character and the formula of the oath by which he has bound himself to obedience are written.[12]

This concept of a *Liber Spiritum* is one that we shall see taken up later on in the history of grimoires.

The next important name that should be mentioned is that of Theophrastus Bombastus von Hohenheim, better known as Paracelsus (1493–1541). Whether Paracelsus was ever directly a pupil of Trithemius has been disputed, but he undoubtedly came under the Abbott's influence and was a member of the same esoteric milieu. Paracelsus was a many-faceted man whose writings range over alchemy, cosmology, medicine and magic. They include a sort of medical grimoire (possibly bogus) entitled *Archidoxis Magica*[13] Primarily he was a physician and an early pioneer of what would now be called the 'holistic' approach to medicine. His medicine rested on what he called his 'four pillars': philosophy, astrology, alchemy and morality. Although his advanced views and stormy temperament outraged his orthodox contemporaries, and he died in poverty in 1541, his influence spread rapidly throughout Europe through his writings and became a tremendous force in the subsequent development of medicine. Curiously, he was the object of a strong cult among the Nazis, which is illustrated by the film *Paracelsus*, made in 1943 with Werner Krauss in the title role.

The synthesis of magical traditions created by such figures as Trithemius, Agrippa and Paracelsus, was carried forward into the period that we now think of as the Rosicrucian era that is roughly the late sixteenth and early seventeenth centuries. Rosicrucianism was a movement of spiritual and intellectual renewal, but it also had a magical element, which is illustrated by a curious work called *The Magical Calender of Tycho Brahe*, published at Frankfurt in 1620, by the famous firm of de Bry, in the form of a large plate covered with sigils, diagrams, symbolic images and lists of correspondences. In the introduction to his English edition in book form, Adam McLean writes:

> The Magical Calender unfolds a synthesis of magical correspondences and symbolism, associated with the magical numbers from one to twelve. This format of compilation is of the greatest value in constructing magical rituals, and one is immediately reminded of S.L. Mathers' 'Book of Correspondences' circulated among members of the R.R. & A.C. [the Rosae Rubeae at Aureae Crucis], the inner orde of the Hermetic Order of the Golden Dawn, which was later published by Aleister Crowley in his own work 'Liber 777'. 777, or rather the Book of correspondences, was indeed used

> as a source for constructing ritual forms, but we have in the *Magical Calender* a text connected with the original Rosicrucian movement, and thus it may be of far greater significance than 777 both historically and esoterically.[14]

Perhaps the most remarkable figure of the Rosicrucian period was not a German but an Englishman, namely John Dee, another person who came under the influence of Trithemius's writings. This seminal figure in the occult tradition and the history of grimoires deserves a chapter to himself.

11.

JOHN DEE AND THE ENOCHIAN WRITINGS

Mention was made earlier of the apocryphal *Book of Enoch*, a work with a magical flavour, which was excluded from the body of canonical literature and preserved only in Ethiopian and Slavonic versions and in a Greek text discovered in the nineteenth century. Although this work remained in obscurity, the reputation of Enoch as a great sage and initiate survived to the extent that some medieval writers even identified him with Hermes.

The concept of Enochian wisdom re-surfaced in a most remarkable form in Elizabethan England, thanks to the extraordinary John Dee (1527-1607), a many-faceted figure who is now regarded as one of the key men of the English Renaissance. Dee was in his fifties, and had already made his mark as a mathematician, geographer and confidant of Queen Elizabeth, when he began to investigate the invisible world of the spirits. Not possessing sufficient clairvoyant powers himself, he employed one Edward Talbot, alias Edward Kelley, as a scryer, that is to say an intermediary who was able to receive messages from the spirits by hearing voices or seeing visions in a mirror or crystal. Between them they 'rediscovered' the divine language of Enochian and produced a series of magical writings supposedly emanating from angelic intelligences. It is debatable whether these writings are grimoires in the strictest sense of the word. Nevertheless, as they have had a seminal influence in western magic up to the present day, they deserve special attention.

Dee and Kelley were a strangely matched pair, yet indispensable to each other in the work that produced the

Enochian material. Kelley supplied the psychic abilities necessary for scrying, while Dee provided the knowledge and intellect that were needed for interpreting and ordering the results. Their partnership began in 1582, and the first scrying session was held on 10 March of that year, when Kelley had a vision of the angel Uriel, who revealed his sigil and gave instructions for the making of a wax tablet, called the Sigillum Emeth, to be used in future evocations. The original tablet, together with a black obsidian scrying mirror and other objects used by Dee and Kelley, can be seen today in the British Museum.

Over the next few sessions Kelley's scrying produced a series of squares made up of familiar angelic names such as Zaphkiel and Zadkiel. From these squares Dee was able to derive new names by reading along the diagonals. Then suddenly Kelley began to produce the Enochian material. On 26 March 1582 he had a vision of a magical book, the pages covered with squares of the kind that they had been dealing with, but this time the letters turned out to be in an unfamiliar alphabet with twenty-one characters. Over the next thirteen months the spirits dictated to Kelley the contents of the book. It exists today in the British Library (Sloane MS 3189) as an untidy manuscript in Kelley's hand entitled the *Liber Logaeth* or *Liber Mysteriorum Sextus et Sanctus*, otherwise known as the *Book from the Speech of God*. What the squares in the book contain is a series of 'calls' or invocations of different supernatural beings.

There are many mysteries about Enochian, and many theories have been advanced about it. Perhaps the most thorough investigation has been carried out by the Australian philologist Dr Donald Laycock in his *Enochian Dictionary*, published in 1978. 'We still do not know', he writes 'whether it is a natural language or an invented language — or whether it is, perhaps the language of the angels, as its originators believed.'[1]

Laycock found that Enochian had a grammar of its own and that certain roots could be identified. The root *om*, for example, meant 'understand or know'. Derived from this were the words *oma* ('understanding'), *omax* ('knowest') and *ixomaxip* ('let it be known').

How did this language come into being? Laycock

believes that it is unlikely to have been invented, in the normal sense of the word, by Dee or Kelley. From what we know of Kelley, its seems unlikely that he was intellectually capable of the complicated feat of inventing a language. Dee, on the other hand, was a high-principled man who would surely have had scruples about such an enterprise. Be that as it may, some people have maintained that Dee did invent Enochian as a means of sending enciphered messages. Now it is suggested, with some plausibility, that Dee did act in the capacity of a secret agent. Furthermore it is known that he possessed a copy of Trithemius's *Steganographia,* which he had bought in Antwerp and about which he wrote enthusiastically in a letter to Sir William Cecil. So it is just possible that some kind of Trithemian system is concealed in the Enochian invocations, but this theory raises more questions than it answers. If Dee was concocting a coding system, why did he need Kelley? Furthermore, as Laycock points out, it would be very difficult to write a text in a strange language in such a way that there was both a straightforward translation (as there is) and an enciphered message. In any case, why bother with a translation at all if the text contained a cipher? These mysteries may never be solved. At any rate, they have contributed to the fascination which Enochian has continued to exert over occultists up to the present day.

The history of Enochian after Dee's death is a remarkable one. Meric Casaubon reproduced some of the Enochian material in his hostile account of Dee's activities, *A True and Faithful Relation* (1659). Shortly after this, Dee's papers came into the hands of the alchemist, astrologer and antiquarian Elias Ashmole (1617–1692) who reconstructed the Enochian magical system and used it in a series of seances between 1671 and 1676. As Ashmole was influential in the founding of English Freemasonry, Laycock speculates that he may have introduced the Enochian system into esoteric Masonry. He certainly played an important role in perpetuating the influence of Enochian within the English occult tradition.

Two hundred years later Enochian surfaced again in the Hermetic Order of the Golden Dawn, whose members used a system called Enochian chess. This is both a game and a divinatory device, combining Enochian magic with Indian four-handed chess. The Enochian system was required study for the Golden Dawn grade of Adeptus Minor.

Aleister Crowley, who went through his magical training in the Golden Dawn, was very fond of the Enochian system. His experiences in using the Enochian calls were published in his journal *The Equinox* and later as a separate book, *The Vision and the Voice*. He also composed additional conjurations in the Enochian language which were published in his edition of MacGregor Mathers' translation of the grimoire known as the *Goetia* or *Lesser Key of Solomon*. Crowley extended the meanings of some of the words and even added new words.

Since then various occult groups have worked with the Enochian system. In England the Order of the Cubic Stone is the principal exponent, while in the United States of America, Anton La Vey's California-based Church of Satan uses the Enochian calls in a form taken from Crowley's version but with some minor variations. For example, where the original has *Iaida* ('The Highest'), La Vey has substituted the name *Saitan*.

An American occultist living near Washington DC once showed me a superb set of Enochian chess pieces which he had made, but warned me, in a manner reminiscent of Mathers' warning about the Abra-Melin demons, that the whole Enochian system was dangerous in the extreme and that those who used it were playing with fire.

Until recently, very little of Dee's work existed in print, but at the time of writing a British esoteric publisher is engaged in producing a five-volume edition of all hitherto unpublished Dee material.[2] It seems likely that the whole subject of Dee, Kelley and the Enochian material will provide scholars and esotericists with a fertile field of study for many decades to come.

12.
The Sixth and Seventh Books of Moses

Solomon and Enoch were not the only biblical figures to whom grimoires were attributed. At a rather later date Moses too was added to the list as the supposed author of some magical texts usually grouped together under the title of the *Sixth and Seventh Books of Moses.* These appear to have originated in Germany, and their history is discussed in an article by Will-Erich Peuckert.[1] Moses, he points out, is said, in the *Acts of the Apostles* (VII, 22) to have been learned in all the wisdom of the Egyptians, and in some of the Greek magical papyri he is quoted as a conjuror of demons. But his name is absent from the list of magi referred to by the medieval and post-medieval occult writers such as Albertus Magnus, Cornelius Agrippa and Trithemius.

Peuckert maintains that interest in the figure of Moses as a magician stems from the Qabalists who sought to extract a secret meaning from the Pentateuch, the first five books of the Old Testament, which tradition attributes to Moses and which are sometimes called the *Five Books of Moses*. He goes on to say that: 'The study of the Qabalah in the non-Jewish world begins with Pico della Mirandola (1463-1494), the great mind of the Florentine Neoplatonic circle. According to him, the Qabalah is the work of the Jewish sage Moses, whose writings he saw as "the inexhaustible source of all wisdom and understanding".' Paracelsus and Aegidius Gutmann saw Moses in a similar light. The latter, in his *Offenbarung göttlicher Majestät* (Revelation of Divine Majesty, 1575), says that God himself wrote the Pentateuch, in the holy language that later came to be called Hebrew, and gave it to Moses. Others maintained that Moses wrote under the inspiration of the Holy Spirit.

As well as receiving the text of the Pentateuch, Moses was also supposed to have received from God knowledge of the secret teaching that lay behind the text. But, according to Pico, Moses did not pass this teaching on to the Hebrews because he felt they were overburdened by the need to understand the Law. Instead he gave it to the Egyptians, who in turn transmitted it to Greek philosophers, such as Plato and Pythagoras.

Writers such as Pico and Paracelsus distinguished between two types of magic: the demonic form, which they considered illicit, and the legitimate kind which consisted of the study of the divine workings of nature. The latter, they maintained, was not only permitted but actually demanded by God. Moses was an adept *par excellence* of this godly magic.

This was the picture of Moses that emerged in the fifteenth and sixteenth centuries, and it was against this background that there appeared the texts known as the *Sixth and Seventh Books of Moses*. A manuscript of the first text was discovered by Peuckert.[2] It bore the title *Rezabla wegesches harez arzas, Rabole or Secrets of the VI Book of Moses*, and its date was given as 1540. It contained conjurations attributed to Moses and written in a gibberish that appeared to be a corrupted form of Hebrew. The following is an example: 'Hazrajeel bai waer wemmchomo mejum mehabeth bischmai rechezem, osischii hamzschii ichamehig gichilo tischo arasjag arisfo vaihachgi.' Peuckert also mentions a printed version of the *Sixth and Seventh Books* together, published in Germany in 1883 as part of the 'Alexander library of magic and arcana'.

It would appear that the title *Sixth and Seventh Books of Moses* is in fact a loose name incorporating a wide range of texts put together by different authors and editors, all of them anxious to capitalize on the name of Moses. Sometimes grimoires appearing under other titles, such as the Faust 'Harrowing of Hell' series, would incorporate material purporting to be quoted from the *Sixth and Seventh Books*. Such is the confusion which besets the whole subject of grimoires. Some of the Moses literature consists of appalling corruptions of plagiarized material, as

Peuckert shows by his analysis of a book published in Braunschweig in 1950 under the title of *The Sixth and Seventh Books of Moses*. Here the names of the Paracelsian elementary spirits have been garbled beyond recognition, so that 'Salamandrae', for example, appears as 'Salomontrae', and 'Silphae' as 'Salpha'.

Yet nonsense of this kind did not prevent *The Sixth and Seventh Books* in their various forms from spreading far and wide. One of the places where they gained a following was in North America, as Herbert Leventhal mentions in his book *In the Shadow of the Enlightenment*, a fascinating study of the survival of occultism and Renaissance science in eighteenth-century America. Leventhal says that most American occultism of that period belonged to a simple and unlearned tradition of witchcraft and folk magic. But he goes on to say: 'There was, however, one group of colonial magic-workers who were very different, who clearly represented a more elaborate and learned form of occultism. These were the magicians, or magi, of the Pennsylvania German community, and their English followers.' One of these Englishmen was Christopher Witt, who joined the German sect headed by Magister Johannes Kelpius and continued to live in Germantown even after the sect was dissolved. 'The learned and scholarly nature of Witt's magic', Leventhal writes, 'is indicated by a 1743 letter from John Bartram to Peter Collinson describing Bartram's visit to a mutual botanizing friend, Christopher Witt: "We went into his study, which was furnished with books containing different kinds of learning; as Philosophy, Natural Magic, Divinity, nay, even Mystical Divinity ..." '[3] These works, he says, included four or five volumes of 'Rosecrution philosophy'. The mention of Rosicrucian works is interesting as an indication of how Rosicrucianism was carried to America by the German pietist immigrants. Kelpius, for example, possessed a manuscript which was an early variant of the *Geheime Figuren der Rosenkreuzer* (Secret Symbols of the Rosicrucians), an alchemical text later published at Altona in 1785.[4]

One of the German magi of this pietist community was George Dresher, who cured victims of witchcraft with the aid of 'a huge black letter manuscript volume, bound with heavy brass clasps'.[5] Another German occultist of the period was Paul Heym, who used his powers to battle with the Indians. He employed a magic circle in his operations, and his methods were drawn partly from the *Sixth and Seventh Books of Moses,* of which he owned a copy. Leventhal describes the *Sixth and Seventh Books* as a 'standard feature of Pennsylvania German magic'.[6] He adds that in America at that time ceremonial magic, apart from the kind connected with treasure-hunting, appears to have been limited to the Pennsylvania Germans. Later, however, the *Sixth and Seventh Books* spread to the mid-West where they were much used by farmers of German origin.

The subsequent history of the pseudo-Moses literature is curious. After being translated into English it was enthusiastically taken up among the black populations of the United States, the Caribbean and West Africa, among whom it is still used. Meanwhile its use continued in its country of birth. A former citizen of the German Democratic Republic told me that the country people of Thuringia were using the *Sixth and Seventh Books* as late as the 1950s.

An American edition of the *Sixth and Seventh Books*[7] and an Indian publication called *The Original Key to the Sixth and Seventh Books of Moses*[8] are both in print at the time of writing. Opening the former, one immediately encounters many familiar names. Here is the ubiquitous Aziel, the black sun of the Chaldeans and the dreaded treasure-finder of the Faust grimoires. In this book Aziel is described, sure enough, as 'a very prompt treasure-spirit of the earth and of the sea'. Here also is Shakespeare's Ariel, 'a very serviceable spirit', and Goethe's Mephistopheles, who 'appears in the form of a youth' and 'is willing to help in all skilled arts'. The material is an extraordinary jumble, taken from many different sources and containing such barbaric evocations as: 'Adus! Baachur! Arbu! Ulu! Frogs, mice, lice and similar vermin arise in our service.' There are also formulae with a biblical flavour. The reader is told, for example, how to use the psalms to bring about different effects. The recital of Psalm

44 will make one safe from one's enemies, while Psalm 52 will serve as a protection against slander. There are illustrations of numerous seals and talismans decorated with, for the most part, rather crudely drawn sigils and Hebrew letters.

In short, the book is an amalgam of flotsam and jetsam from a number of different traditions. But it is precisely such flotsam and jetsam that are often carried the furthest distance in time and space. The *Sixth and Seventh Books,* linking as they do the Kansas farmer, the Caribbean islander and the Chaldean sages of old, are a remarkable case in point.

13.
Magic in the Nineteenth Century

The 'golden age' of magic lasted, as we have seen, from about the mid fifteenth to the late seventeenth century. Then, during the eighteenth century, the 'Age of Enlightenment', magic and its apologists became less conspicuous. Although esoteric traditions were perpetuated among certain groups, the general spirit of classical objectivity and rational enquiry was out of tune with the occult world view. But before the eighteenth century was out the beginnings of a reaction could be discerned in the form of what came to be called Romanticism, a movement whose influence was felt in many spheres, from literature and music to architecture and the visual arts. This created a favourable setting for a revival of occultism.

It was in the period when this new spirit was emerging that an occult bookseller named John Denley set up business in London with a shop in Catherine Street, Covent Garden. Denley, who kept his shop going from about the 1790s until around 1840, was himself an impressive occult scholar, and he became a well-known figure among those interested in esoteric literature. He appears, for example, in the introduction to Edward Bulwer-Lytton's 'Rosicrucian' novel *Zanoni,* which describes his shop as being filled with works on alchemy, astrology, Qabalah and related subjects.

Among Denley's customers was one Francis Barrett, who plays an important role in the history of occult writing on account of his book *The Magus, or Celestial Intelligencer,* which appeared in 1801. In compiling *The Magus,* Barrett was allowed by Denley to make free use of the latter's remarkable collection of books, and Barrett succeeded in putting together a wide-ranging compendium of occult lore from the volumes on Denley's dusty shelves. When *The Magus* was published Barrett offended Denley by neglecting to give him a copy, but Denley later had his revenge. Barrett fell into financial difficulties and sold his stock of copies to another bookseller named Lackington, along with the plates of the book and his copyright in it. These were then bought by Denley who evidently decided to teach Barrett a lesson by hanging on to them for some years. Subsequently the material passed into the hands of the occultist Frederick Hockley.[1]

About Barrett himself very little is known. His portrait on the frontispiece of the book shows a youngish, rather handsome man with an untidy mop of hair. He is described as a 'Student in Chemistry, Metaphysicks, Natural & Occult Philosophy &c. &c.' At the time the book was published he was living at No. 99 Norton Street, in the Marylebone district of London, where he gave lessons in the magical arts.

Timothy d'Arch Smith, in his introduction to a modern reprint of *The Magus*, points out the links between the magical revival and the Gothic revival, which began in the late eighteenth century as part of the general trend towards Romanticism:

> The gothic philosophy offered a gentle and reassuring retreat from the all-too-blatant and actual horrors portrayed so vividly by Hogarth and from the starchy classicism of Hanoverian days. Horace Walpole and William Beckford, to name but two, went a step further and attempted to adopt the gothic way of life in the vast edifices they had erected at Strawberry Hill and at Fonthill, and it is no surprise to learn that, at Beckford's Abbey, whispers were heard of magical practices within that enormous pile. For medieval magic and the gothic went hand in hand, and along with the shivers so delightfully imparted by the novelists down the spines of their young female readers, went a genuine straining after higher things. Magic was in the air, a return to the practices and philosophies of the medieval adepts was demanded. It was time for the true Rosicrucian, in the person of Francis Barrett, to come into the open and to show the way.

> Barrett's *Magus* is unique in being the only attempt — at a time when interest was ripe — to revive the mysteries of magic, and he clearly spent long hours toiling over translations of Qabalistic lore which had never before been translated into English or which were issued in the seventeenth century and were then, as now, of the last rarity.[2]

The question arises how Barrett came to be inspired to write *The Magus* and who, if anyone, introduced him to magic. Was he perhaps part of some occult coterie in London? If so, who were his seniors in the group? We can only guess who Barrett's mentors were, but one of them might have been Dr Ebenezer Sibly (1752–1799), author of a treatise called *The Complete Illustration of the Celestial Art of Astrology* (published in four parts of which the first appeared in 1784). Though mainly astrological, this work contained a lengthy dissertation on magic. Sibly also wrote an astro-medical textbook, *The Key to Physick and the Occult Science,* and his brother Manoah, also an astrologer, translated two of the works by Placidus. Sibly was an active Freemason, and it seems quite likely that he was the centre or at least a member of a circle of like-minded people who kept the esoteric tradition going in the eighteenth century. It also seems possible that the young Barrett would have come under his influence.

Turning to the text of Barrett's *Magus,* we find that the work is a curious mixture of barbarism and spirituality, naïvety and sophistication. Barrett writes as one who has clearly steeped himself in the old grimoires and Qabalistic writings but also as a practising magician.

The work is divided into two books. In Part I of the first book, dealing with Natural Magic, Barrett is at his most credulous. He believes, for example, that, 'the toad hath a natural aversion to man; and this sealed image, or idea of hatred, he carries in his head, eyes, and most powerfully throughout his whole body.'[3] And he goes on to say that, 'the poison of the plague is subdued by the poison of the toad, not by an action primarily destructive, but by a secondary action; as the pestilent idea of hatred or terror extinguishes the ferment, by whose mediation the poison of the plague subsists, and proceeds to infect ... Therefore the opposition of the amulet formed from the body, &c., of the toad, takes away and prevents the baneful and most horrible effects ... of the plague'.[4]

In Part II of the first book, he turns to talismanic magic, discussing in detail the power and significance of the numbers from one to twelve, including tables of correspondences which anticipate Crowley's 777. He also describes a series of planetary images similar to those listed by Agrippa.

One of his most interesting chapters is entitled 'Of the Spirit of the World', and here he refers to a very ancient concept that greatly fascinated the Renaissance occultists. 'This spirit', writes Barrett, 'is, in the same manner, in the body of the world, as our spirit is in our bodies, for as the powers of our soul are communicated to the members of the body by the medium of the spirit, so also the virtue of the soul of the world is diffused, throughout all things, by the medium of the universal spirit.' In this spirit, 'are all *generative and seminal virtues*. For which cause the alchymist endeavours to separate this spirit from gold and silver ...'[5] This concept of a spirit residing in the coarse matter of the world links Barrett with the Gnostics.

The second book begins with a discussion of what Barrett calls 'magnetism' by which he means the mysterious force that, for example, links a glass of wine to the original vine from which it came, or by contrast causes certain things to be repugnant to one another. 'Upon this principle of sympathy and antipathy', he writes, 'is founded that spiritual power which tends to things and objects remote one from the other,'[6] that is to say, magic. In another part Barrett writes that the knowledge of magical power has lain dormant in man since the Fall, but that it can be aroused by the 'Art of the Cabala' and that man 'by his magical faculty ... is able to subdue the magical virtues of all other things.'[7] These again are Gnostic concepts.

When he comes to the section on ceremonial magic, Barrett introduces the reader to numerous demons and names of power, describes magical equipment and gives detailed instructions for the casting of circles and for invocation. Many of the drawings of demons and sigils that illustrate the book were done by Barrett himself.

Barrett's sources are often easy to recognize. In Book II,

for example, he gives a detailed description of how to make and consecrate a *Book of Spirits* for use in conjurations. This appears to have been taken in large part from the pseudo-Agrippa's *Fourth Book of Occult Philosophy* (see my quote on page 90).

In the wake of Barrett's *Magus* came another compilation of magical and occult lore, this time mingled with astrological prophecies and fiction and presented so as to appeal to a more popular readership. This was *The Astrologer in the Nineteenth Century or: The Master Key of Futurity, and Guide to Ancient Mysteries, being a Complete System of Occult Philosophy*. Its authors were described as 'Members of the Mercurii' and were listed as 'Raphael, the Metropolitan Astrologer, the editor of the Prophetic Almanack, and other Sidereal Artists of First-Rate Eminence'. Raphael was in fact a man with the more prosaic name of Robert Cross Smith (1795–1832), and the Mercurii was an occult society which he founded. He later started up an immensely successful periodical called *The Prophetic Messenger*. Interestingly, Smith was a friend of William Blake and drew up the poet's horoscope.

The Astrologer in the Nineteenth Century was published in several editions by the London firm of Knight and Lacey whose list also included such sober titles as *A Descriptive History of the Steam Engine, The Cabinet-Makers' Guide* and *Practical Chemical Mineralogy.*

In the introduction the authors declare: 'As to the more *mystical* part of the work, the theory of *magic, rites, charms, and incantations,* they are inserted merely to complete the development of occult studies, formerly pursued by our forefathers, who firmly believed therein — we ourselves, however, advocate them not, but leave them to those who delight in the terrific, and the horribly sublime.[8]

Despite this disclaimer, Raphael and the Mercurii must have known that many readers would take the magical part of the book seriously and even use it for practical purposes. The section on 'Magic Ceremonies, Charms and Incantations, comprising the Ancient Practice of Raising Spirits' is prefaced by a note to the effect that it was compiled from a selection of ancient and modern works on the subject and from original manuscripts. Quoting from Agrippa, Wier, Barrett, Trithemius and others, Raphael gives an outline of the angelic hierarchies, information on 'Mysterious Writing' and 'Cabalistical Words of Great Efficacy', and a who's who of spirits with their descriptions, rulerships and attributions. The book has some vivid illustrations of the spirits. One, for example, shows Oriens, King of the East, who 'appeareth with a fair and feminine countenance, and a goodly crown upon his head; he rideth upon an elephant, having before him numbers of musical instruments.'

Any reader who wished could have used this text as a manual for magical work. The section on invoking spirits, for example, contains detailed instructions and formulae. 'The place chosen', the author says, 'must be secluded, solitary, and isolated from the resort of men.' And an intriguing footnote states: 'The late learned Mr R. Cosway, R.A. hired a room, which he kept always consecrated for the purpose of raising spirits. On the floor he had the magic circle drawn, and it was never entered by any idle or curious intruder. This, we have been assured by a gentleman, who was an intimate friend of Mr Cosway, was actually the case.'[9] If the report is true, it is fascinating to know that at that era a member of the royal academy was engaged in the invocation of spirits. The same Mr Cosway was the owner of some precious magical manuscripts, one of which, according to a footnote, passed into the hands of the Mercurii, and many of the instructions in it are quoted in the book. Here, for example, is part of the formula for raising Egin, King of the North:

> I conjure thee, Egin, Rex Borealis, and also charge thee that thou appear here before me, and before this circle, by the sufferance of Almighty God, and by the virtue of his passion and other sentences which here shall be rehearsed, to bind and constrain thee.
>
> I conjure thee, Egin, by the Father, the Son, and the Holy Ghost, and by the heavens, the air, the earth and the sea, and by all that therein is contained, that thou come shortly and appear to me and my fellows, not terrible nor fearful, but in mild and peaceable form, without hurt of envy to any of us.
>
> I conjure thee, Egin, by all the holy words that God spake in the creation of the world, and by all creatures visible and invisible, and by the four elements, and by the virtue of heaven, and by all the holy words that God spoke unto

> Moses, and to all other prophets, and by the incarnation, passion, death, and resurrection, of the mild and ineffable saviour of all mankind.[10]

An accompanying illustration shows Egin riding a winged dragon.

Similar instructions are given for raising Oberion, described as a 'mighty spirit' who is chiefly under the dominion of the sun and moon and who 'appears in great pomp and terror, generally in the form of a scaly monster, the face of a woman, and a royal crown upon his head, attended by innumerable and countless legions.[11] Again, there is a grotesque illustration of the demon.

A further section deals with necromancy and the raising of the spirits of the dead. An illustration to this shows John Dee's colleague, Edward Kelley, raising a ghost in a churchyard.

One of the manuscripts quoted from is a translation of a Latin Qabalistic treatise allegedly written by the painter Rubens and annexed to a work on the proportions of the human figure. The quotation deals with the hexagram or seal of Solomon. Rubens writes that perfection in the world will come:

> When this character, *denoting hieroglyphically* the spiritual signature both of David and Solomon; denoting the two eternal principles *in union;* denoting the creation of the *third principle;* denoting the *six* working properties of eternal nature in their everlasting *rest;* denoting fire and water in an harmonious union, denoting the two tinctures restored in ONE, who is ALL in ALL, or without whom there can be nothing; denoting that all whatever was, or is, or shall be, is of, and through, and to, that ONE; denoting *almost the whole* instance of time and eternity, as the same, in our age, is laid open by Jacob Behmen, that blessed instrument in the hands of the Spirit of God; on which account, I may justly call this seal or character *prophetical* ... when this character, I say, spiritualized, and only with *addition of a cross,* which is not expressed therein directly (and no wonder that it was not in those days), shall be the broad seal, not only of the eternal King of kings, but also of every one of his subjects.[12]

This Rubens treatise was another of the manuscripts that had been owned by Richard Cosway.

Another of the intriguing footnotes in *The Astrologer in the Nineteenth Century* refers to the seventeenth-century clergyman and philosopher, Dr Francis Lee. Dr Lee is stated to have been a promoter of charities of all kinds and a confidant of Peter the Great of Russia, 'for whom, by request, he wrote, in the year 1696, "Proposals for the right framing of his Government".' The note goes on:

> Dr Lee was a member of 'The Philadelphian Society': I therefore recommend a perusal of the 'Theosophical Transactions', by that Society (1 vol. small 4to. 1697), as it contains the most erudite and profound disquisitions ever written, both scientific and philosophic, as well as theosophic and divine magic. This singular work has been very rare for the last fifty years, and, as a proof of that, the copy belonging to the late Mr Cosway was sold by a bookseller (Duke Street, Manchester Square), to a friend of mine, for ten guineas.[13]

One of the most detailed sections of *The Astrologer in the Nineteenth Century* concerns the making of talismans, charms and magical implements. For example, a quotation from 'a rare German alchemical manuscript in the possession of the Mercurii' gives instructions for making a device called the Urim and Thummim, a kind of divinatory mirror whose framework has to be made of a substance called electrum magicum. This is produced by a complicated alchemical process lasting several days and involving gold, antimony, saltpetre, quicksilver, copper and lead.[14] The same material can also be used to make a magic bell for invoking spirits.

While Barrett, Raphael and others were busy reviving magic in England, a similar and even more vigorous revival was taking place in France. Here also grimoires appeared in the form of compilations or digests or earlier occult writings. An example was Lenain's *La Science cabalistique ou l'art de connaître les bons génies*, published at Amiens in 1823. This book, which relies heavily on Agrippa, Kircher, Reuchlin and others, is a clearly-written presentation, which stresses the higher side of magic. It includes an interesting chapter on the spirits of the third degree, that is those of the elements: gnomes (earth), who are guardians of mines and precious stones; nymphs (water); sylphs (air) and salamanders (fire). Fire is the master element of the four, and salamanders are 'the most beautiful and the most perfect of the elemental creatures because they are composed of the most subtle parts of fire, combined and organized by the action of the universal fire, which is the principle of all the movements of nature'. Lenain continues: 'Thus the man who wishes to regenerate himself and recover his primal dignity and ascendancy over the elements should purify and exalt the fire element that is in him.'[15] He then gives a curious recipe for concentrating the universal fire in a glass sphere by the use of concave mirrors and thereby exalting the fire within the operator and gaining the allegiance of the salamanders.

As the nineteenth century progressed, France increasingly became a hotbed of occult activity. After Lenain came such works as Eusèbe Salverte's *Des sciences occultes ou essai sur la magie, les prodigues et les miracles* (Paris, 1829), not exactly a grimoire, but a book which helped to feed public interest in occult literature. As for grimoires proper, many were published in France in the nineteenth century. The *Grimoire du Pape Honorius* appeared several times — one edition, for example, was published at Lille in 1840. The *Grand Grimoire, ou l'art de commander les esprits célestes* appeared at Paris in 1845, and various editions of the *Grand Albert* and *Petit Albert* were also issued during the course of the century.

Many occult streams were running through France at this time. There was a growing interest in the Tarot as a result of Court de Gebelin's enthusiastic discourse on it in *Le Monde Primitif* (1773-1784). There was animal magnetism, Freemasonry of the most exotic kinds, Martinism, Qabalism, alchemy. One man, more than any other, was responsible for drawing these streams together: Alphonse-Louis Constant, better known under his adopted Hebrew name of Eliphas Lévi (1810–1875).

Lévi was mainly a theoretician of the occult, though he did occasionally practise magic, as witness his evocation of the Greek sage Apollonius of Tyana on a visit to London in 1854, which he describes in his *Dogme de la Magie.* His books are not grimoires as such, but some of them could be used as grimoires by extracting the practical details and formulae which Lévi often includes. An example is his chapter on the conjuration of the four elements in his *Rituel de la Haute Magie* which includes prayers to the creatures of the elements, the sylphs, undines, salamanders and gnomes. In another chapter, dealing with necromancy, he comments interestingly on the types of books to be used in evoking the dead:

> The ceremony should begin with a prayer suited to the genius of the spirit about to be invoked and one which would be approved by himself if he still lived. For example, it would be impossible to evoke Voltaire by reciting prayers in the style of St Bridget. For the great men of antiquity, we may use the Hymns of Cleanthes or Orpheus, with the oath terminating the Golden Verses of Pythagoras. In our evocation of Apollonius, we used the Magical Philosophy of Patricius for the Ritual, containing the doctrines of Zoroaster and the writings of Hermes Trismegistus. We recited the Nuctemeron of Apollonius in Greek with a loud voice and added a Conjuration beginning: 'Let the Father of all be Counsellor and thrice-great Hermes guide.'[16]

For the evocation of spirits belonging to religions issued from Judaism, the following Kabalistic Invocation of Solomon should be used, either in Hebrew or in any other tongue with which the spirit in question is known to have been familiar:

> Powers of the Kingdom, be ye under my left foot and in my right hand! Glory and Eternity, take me by the two shoulders, and direct me in the paths of victory! Mercy and Justice, be ye the equilibrium and splendour of my life! Intelligence and Wisdom, crown me! Spirits of Malkuth, lead me betwixt the two Pillars upon which rests the edifice of the whole temple! Angels of Netzah and Hod, establish me upon the cubic stone of Yesod! O Gedulael! O Geburael! O Tiphereth! Binaël, be ye my love! Ruach Hochmael, be thou my light! Be that which thou art and thou shalt be, O Ketheriel! Ishim, assist me in the name of Saddai! Cherubim, be my strength in the name of Adonai! Beni-Elohim, be my brethren in the name of the Son, and by the powers of Zebaoth! Eloim, do battle for me in the name of Tetragrammaton! Melachim, protect me in the name of Yod He Vav He! Seraphim, cleanse my love in the name of Elvoh! Hasmalim, enlighten me with the splendours of Eloi and Shekinah! Aralim, act! Ophanim, revolve and shine! Hajoth a Kadosh, cry, speak, roar, bellow! Kadosh, Kadosh, Kadosh,

> Shaddai, Adonai, Jotchavah, Eieazereie! Hallelujah, Hallelujah, Hallelujah. Amen.[17]

Lévi acquired many followers both inside and outside France. One of them was the odd British scholar and occultist Kenneth Mackenzie, a leading light in the English Rosicrucian revival and an important influence in shaping the milieu from which the Hermetic Order of the Golden Dawn emerged in 1887.

Too much has been written about the Golden Dawn to warrant a full account of its history here, but the bare facts are as follows. It was founded by Dr William Wynn Westcott (1848–1925), Dr William Robert Woodman (1828–1891) and Samuel Liddell MacGregor Mathers (1854–1918). Mathers, a colourful character who claimed Jacobite ancestry and used the title Comte de Glenstrae, was the main architect of the order.

Like many similar phenomena, the Golden Dawn started with a document — not exactly a grimoire but a manuscript of about sixty leaves written in a secret alphabet evidently taken from the *Poligraphiae* of Trithemius. This manuscript is said to have been discovered at a bookstall in the Farringdon Road. When translated, it was found to contain the outlines of rituals used by a society called the Hermetic Order of the Golden Dawn. Westcott asked Mathers to expand the rituals into a complete scheme of initiation, which Mathers did with great skill, drawing on his wide knowledge of the Qabalah and the occult tradition. The result was a magical system of tremendous force and coherence.

The most famous member of the Golden Dawn was Aleister Crowley (1875–1947), the stormy petrel of the occult world, who joined the order in 1898. Shortly after this the order split and Crowley went his own way, disillusioned with Mathers.

Both Mathers and Crowley were remarkable men in their own ways. Mathers created an order of such vitality that its impact is being felt today perhaps more strongly than ever. Crowley, drawing on the Golden Dawn tradition, Tantric sex magic and his own visions, also created a teaching of great force. Both of them also produced and inspired writings which are still being avidly read by students of the occult.

14.
THE BOOK OF ABRA-MELIN

MacGregor Mathers was responsible for bringing out editions of a number of grimoires based on his research in manuscript archives in London and Paris. These include the *Greater Key of Solomon* and the *Grimoire of Armadel*. But probably the most important work that he brought to light was *The Book of the Sacred Magic of Abra-Melin the Mage,* 'as delivered by Abraham the Jew unto his son Lamech, AD 1458'. It was found by Mathers in the Bibliothèque de l'Arsenal in Paris, a remarkable library which grew from the private collection of the Marquis de Paulny, founded in the eighteenth century, and still flourishes on the right bank of the Seine near the Place de la Bastille.

In his introduction, Mathers writes as follows:

> Many years ago I heard of the existence of this manuscript from a celebrated occultist, since dead; and more recently my attention was again called to it by my personal friend, the well-known French author, lecturer and poet, Jules Bois, whose attention has been for some time turned to occult subjects. My first-mentioned informant told me that it was known both to Bulwer Lytton and Eliphas Lévi, that the former had based part of his description of the Rosicrucian Sage Mejnour on that of Abra-Melin, while the account of the so-called Observatory of Sir Philip Derval in the 'Strange Story' was to an extent copied from and suggested by that of the Magical Oratory and Terrace, given in the Eleventh Chapter of the Second Book of this present work. Certainly also the manner of instruction applied by Mejnour in 'Zanoni' to the Neophyte Glyndon, together with the test of leaving him alone in his abode, to go on a short journey and

then returning unexpectedly, is closely similar to that employed by Abra-Melin to Abraham, with this difference, that the latter successfully passed through that test, while Glyndon failed. It would also be especially such experiments as those described at length in the Third Book, which the author of the 'Strange Story' had in view when he makes Sir Philip Derval in the MS history of his life speak of certain books describing occult experiments, some of which he had tried and to his surprise found succeed.

This rare and unique manuscript of the Sacred Magic of Abra-Melin from which the present work is translated, is a French translation from the orginal Hebrew of Abraham the Jew. It is in the style of script usual at about the end of the seventeenth and beginning of the eighteenth centuries, and is apparently by the same hand as another MS of the Magic of Picatrix also in the 'Bibliothèque de l'Arsenal'. I know of no other existing copy or replica of this Sacred Magic of Abra-Melin, not even in the British Museum, whose enormous collection of Occult Manuscripts I have very thoroughly studied ...

This system of Sacred Magic Abraham acknowledges to have received from the Mage Abra-Melin; and claims to have himself personally and actually wrought most of the wonderful effects described in the Third Book, and many others besides.

Who then was this Abraham the Jew? It is possible, though there is no mention of this in the MS, that he was a descendant of that Abraham the Jew who wrote the celebrated Alchemical work on twenty-one pages of bark or papyrus, which came into the hands of Nicholas Flamel, and by whose study the latter is said eventually to have attained the possession of the 'Stone of the Wise'. The only remains of the Church of Saint Jacques de la Boucherie which exists at the present day, is the tower, which stands near the Place du Châtelet, about ten minutes' walk from the Bibliothèque de l'Arsenal; and there is yet a street near this tower which bears the title of 'Rue Nicolas Flamel', so that his memory still survives in Paris, together with that of the Church close to which he lived, and to which, after the attainment of the Philosopher's Stone, he and his wife Pernelle caused a handsome peristyle to be erected.

From his own account, the author of the present work appears to have been born in AD 1362, and to have written this manuscript for his son, Lamech, in 1458, being then in his ninety-sixth year. That is to say, that he was the

> contemporary both of Nicholas Flamel and Pernelle, and also of the mystical Christian Rosencreutz, the founder of the celebrated Rosicrucian Order or Fraternity in Europe. Like the latter, he appears to have been very early seized with the desire of obtaining Magical Knowledge; like him and Flamel, he left his home and travelled in search of the Initiated Wisdom; like them both, he returned to become a worker of wonders ...[1]

Abra-Melin is divided into three books. In the first the author gives general advice and recounts his journey to Egypt where he acquired wisdom from a sage named Abra-Melin, and his subsequent travels around Europe and meetings with various magicians. The second book consists of detailed instructions for a magical operation whose aim is to attain divine wisdom and magical powers through contact with one's Guardian Angel. The reader is cautioned against the dangers of beginning the operation without being able to carry it through and is told that he must be in good health, that his life must be tranquil and his habits temperate. The author emphasizes the spiritual nature of the work and condemns the debased grimoires. 'All the books' he writes 'which treat of Characters, Extravagant Figures, Circles, Convocations, Conjurations, Invocations, and other like matters, even although one may see some effect thereby, should be rejected, being works full of Diabolical Inventions.'[2] The third book gives instructions on the use of the magical powers attained in the second book and consists chiefly of spells written out in the form of magical squares.

What distinguishes *Abra-Melin* from most other grimoires is that it does away with a lot of the heavy paraphernalia and complicated procedures traditional to western magic. The system of planetary hours, for example, is decried as an absurdity, and the magician is not required to cast circles or make talismans. The procedure laid down is, however, strict and arduous. First it is necessary to construct an oratory in a suitable place.

> He who commenceth this Operation in solitude can elect a place according to his pleasure; where there is a small wood, in the midst of which you shall make a small Altar, and you

> shall cover the same with a hut (or shelter) of fine branches, so that the rain may not fall thereon and extinguish the Lamp and the Censer. Around the Altar at a distance of seven paces you shall prepare a hedge of flowers, plants and green shrubs, so that it may divide the entrance into two parts.

If, however, the magician lives in a town, he is instructed as follows:

> Ye shall choose an Apartment which hath a Window, joined unto the which shall be an uncovered Terrace (or Balcony), and a Lodge (or small room or hut) covered with a roof, but so that there may be on every side windows whence you may be able to see in every direction and whence you may enter into the Oratory. In the which place [the terace or balcony] the Evil spirits shall be able to appear, since they cannot appear within the Oratory itself ...
>
> The Oratory should always be clear and clean swept, and the flooring should be of wood, of white pine; in fine, this place should be so well and carefully prepared that one may judge it to be a place destined unto prayer.[3]

The magician must also be equipped with magical vestments: a shirt or tunic of linen and a robe 'of Crimson or Scarlet Silk with Gold'. In addition he must make sacred oil and incense and a wand of almond wood.

As to the operation itself, this lasts for six months. During the first two months the magician prays every morning, studies the scriptures and leads a simple and frugal life. During the second two months he prays morning and evening and the prayers are prolonged; furthermore he must now fast every Sabbath eve. In the last two months the operation intensifies, and the magician now prays three times a day, using prescribed words and procedures. At a certain point during this time, if all has gone according to plan, the moment that the magician has been waiting for arrives:

> You shall see your Guardian Angel appear unto you in unequalled beauty; who also will converse with you, and speak in words so full of affection and of goodness, and with such sweetness, that no human tongue could express the same ... he will show unto you the True Wisdom and Holy

> Magic, and also wherein you have erred in your Operation, and how thenceforward you should proceed in order to overcome the Evil Spirits, and finally arrive at your desired ends.[4]

Having obtained the 'Knowledge and Conversation of the Holy Guardian Angel', which in psychological terms can be seen as the higher self, the magician now proceeds to summon the Evil Spirits and command their obedience, first the 'Four Superior Princes', Lucifer, Leviathan, Satan and Belial, then 'Eight Sub-Princes', Astaroth, Magoth, Asmodeus, Beelzebub, Oriens, Paimon, Ariton and Amaymon. Psychologically this can be interpreted as a confrontation with the unassimilated archetypes and shadow complexes which can be brought under conscious control once the higher self has been contacted.

The third book deals with the application of the magical powers gained during the operation. It consists largely of magical squares, each one for a specific purpose. Some are for divination, for example, 'to know all things Past and Future in general', 'to know the Secrets of War', 'to know true and false Friends'. Others are used to cause the appearance of angels and familiar spirits in different forms. This part of the book is therefore addressed to the fully integrated individual who is able to confront forces inside and outside himself without flinching.

Those who have undertaken the Abra-Melin Operation include Aleister Crowley who carried it out at his house Boleskine on Loch Ness. He used one of the north-facing rooms of the house as an oratory and also built a lodge for the demons to congregate in. Unfortunately Astaroth, Magoth, Asmodeus and the rest of the demonic horde escaped from the lodge and began to invade the house, with disastrous consequences. A teetotal coachman began to suffer from *delirium tremens*, a workman on the estate went mad and tried to kill Crowley, and a butcher in the village cut himself fatally with a meat cleaver after Crowley had jotted down the names of two Abra-Melin demons on a meat bill. Crowley, undeterred, proceeded with the operation and eventually, as he claimed, gained the knowledge and conversation of his Holy Guardian Angel.

The Abra-Melin system must not be tampered with by the faint-hearted, and it is worth quoting a cautionary tale which appeared in a letter from one H. Campbell written to the *Occult Review* in December, 1929.

> Desiring some information which I could not get in any ordinary way, I resorted to the System of Abramelin, and to this end prepared a copy of the necessary Talisman, perfecting it to the best of my ability with my little stock of knowledge. The ritual performed, I proceeded to clear my 'place of working'. A little knowledge is a dangerous thing; my ritual was imperfect and I only rendered the Talisman useless without in any way imparing the activities of the entity invoked. This looks like nothing else than gross carelessness on my part; and to a certain extent this is true — but the point I wish to make is this, that my knowledge of this particular system, and therefore my ritual, were imperfect; and in any case, I had been shown no method of combating this particular entity when once aroused. Now note the results.
>
> Unfortunately I have no account of the date when these occurrences began, but the first hint of trouble must have come on or about March 3, 1927. I can guess the date with fair accuracy because, as I was to learn, the manifestations were always strongest about the new moon, and after I had gone to sleep. Upon this occasion I can remember waking up suddenly with a vague feeling of terror oppressing me; yet it was no ordinary nightmare terror, but an imposed emotion that could be thrown off by an effort of the will. This passed almost as soon I stood up, and I thought no more about it.
>
> Again on April 2, or thereabouts, I was troubled by the same feeling, but regarded it as nothing more than a severe nightmare, though the fact that my sleep was distorted towards the time of the new moon had occurred to me; while as full moon drew on, the nights were peaceful again.
>
> The new moon of May 1 brought a recurrence of the trouble. This time it was very much more powerful, and necessitated an almost intolerable effort of will to cast it off. Also it was about this time that I first saw the entity which was rapidly obsessing me. It was not altogether unlovely to look at. Its eyes were closed and it was bearded, with long flowing hair. It seemed a blind force slowly waking to activity.
>
> Now there are three points which I must make quite clear

before I proceed. In the first place, I was never attacked twice in the same night. Secondly, when I speak of physical happenings, the smashing of glass and voices, they were never, with one absolutely inexplicable exception, actual, but pure obsessions; and this leads to the third point. Not one of these incidents happened while I was asleep. Always I found myself awake with the terror upon me and struggling violently to cast off the spell. I have had nightmares before, but no nightmare that I have ever had could hold my mind in its grip for minutes at a time as this thing did, or send me plunging through a ten-foot-high window to the ground below.

The first indication I had that these visitations were absolutely out of the ordinary course of events came on May 30. About midnight I was suddenly awakened by a voice calling loudly, 'Look out', and at once I became aware of a red serpent coiling and uncoiling itself under my bed, and reaching out onto the floor with its head. Just as it was about to attack me I jumped through my window, and came to earth among the rose bushes below, fortunately with no more damage than a badly bruised arm.

After this there was absolute peace until June 30, when the real climax came. I had seen the thing again on the night of the new moon, and had noticed considerable changes in its appearance. Especially it seemed far more active, while its long hair had changed into serpent heads. The night after I was awakened by a violent noise and jumped out of bed. I then saw the noise was caused by a great red obelisk which crashed through the west wall of my room and leaned against the wall at the east end, smashing both that and window to pieces but missing my bed, which was in an alcove to the left of its path. In its transit it had smashed all the mirrors, and the floor and top of my bed were strewn with broken glass and fragments of wood. This time the obsession must have lasted some minutes, I dared not move for fear of cutting myself, and to reach the matches — wherein, I knew, lay safety — I had to lean across the bed and again risk the glass. Yet in my heart I knew that all this was false, but had no power to move. I could only stand there, incapable, looking at the shattered room in a state of hopeless terror.

And now comes the most extraordinary part of the whole business. When I finally mastered the obsession, I went to bed again dead tired, and I know that the only sound I made that night was jumping to the floor, also my room is at least a hundred yards from the rest of my family, yet next morning

> at breakfast I was asked what was the terrible noise in my room during the night.
>
> After that I realised that the game was up. I had not taken these occurrences lying down, but I knew that it was impossible for me to try and control the force which I had set in motion. In desperation I turned to a good friend, who, I was aware, knew much of these things. She did not hesitate, but came at once to my assistance, and from that day to the present the trouble has absolutely gone from me.
>
> Such is the case; and I only hope it may warn those who are contemplating my folly to treat with the greatest of care any printed systems of magic, and not to use them at all unless they have the fullest control over the entities invoked.

Less violent results attended another Abra-Melin operation carried out in 1973 by a magician calling himself 'Georges Chevalier', whose diary of the operation was published under the title of *The Sacred Magician*. Chevalier records powerfully the alternating sensations of joy and anguish that he felt during the operation, which he succeeded in carrying through to its conclusion. Here is how he describes the summoning of the four princes towards the end of the operations:

> Having robed myself, I fell to my knees and prayed as directed in the Book and, naturally, by my heart. I shortly felt my Angel's presence and heard his words. How amazing yet natural to write all this ... I stood, wand in my right hand and Psalm XIC in my left hand, and called the four princes. Within a few minutes they came, only twice attempting to frighten me, once with a great whooshing sound that burnt my back (and the little doggy came past) and later pretending they were behind and threatening me. And then they did each take the correct oath. The marvel was that my Angel had so well prepared me over the last six months that the whole thing was done with the most great and surprising ease. He had made me so that my attitude was almost impeccable and the four princes knew it was not worth their while to chide or insult or seek to ensnare me. Psalm XIC holds great mysteries that gave me much strength and understanding. Though I was to constrain the four princes to appear in the shape of men, they took no shape and for a while this confused me. I looked to my Angel for explanation and confirmation, and he told me that, as I knew, they were not of gross matter and if

they appeared in a human shape, it would only be one of a cliché pulled from kama-manasic matter of which I had no need ...[5]

Another contemporary occultist, Lionel Snell, carried out the Abra-Melin working while staying at a cottage in Redbourn, Hertfordshire, in the summer of 1977. He too completed the operation and found that it brought about profound, though subtle, changes in him. When I asked him to describe these changes in writing, he gave me an eloquent account, which I quote in conclusion to this chapter:

It was a voyage of self-discovery. Six months might not seem a very long time to dedicate yourself wholeheartedly to a single project; but when that project is one that would be judged as a worthless illusion in the eyes of the world, then six months is plenty of time to wonder what you *really* want. Don't forget, you have already sworn a vow to complete the six months.

And at the end when nothing happens? ... By then every event is a message, and the lack of a conclusion seems as much a proof that the operation has not finished as a proof of failure. In subsequent years everyday events took on a dramatic significance. An experienced old friend told me on several occasions: 'Everyone who plays the Holy Guardian Angel Game first evokes his own ego. Only once that illusion is recognised and conquered can the real contact come.' Each time I agreed — it is so easy to see the truth of this in other lives. The third time he said it the thought crossed my mind: 'I wish I had found something as exciting as a bloated ego image at the end of it all.' A year later I saw him again, and he said the same. I thought the same. On the way home I asked myself what form my bloated ego image would have taken. A blank. Then the sudden awareness that my ego image was not the Great Sage, the Guru, the Man of Power ... it was the Lovable Failure, the Chaplinesque figure who fails and presents no threat and so can safely accept love from everyone. I stopped the car by the roadside and sat in amazement. Abra-Melin had delivered my ego figure right on schedule. With this realisation another step was taken.

You see, in the last few days of the work the Holy Guardian Angel introduces you to the Demons one by one, and you have to subdue them with your wand. My Demons have been introduced to me one by one, but it has taken years not days. This is perhaps because my rationalist education refuses to recognise a Demon for what it is. In the above example it took about four years even to see that I had been brought face to face with a Demon — and that is only the first step towards subduing it. Other demons have been quicker and more obviously recognisable. The operation goes on.

15.

THE LITERATURE OF WITCHCRAFT AND OTHER MODERN GRIMOIRES

As my purpose is to deal with the transmission of magic through written texts, I have said little so far about the orally transmitted traditions of folk magic — traditions which in the Christian world have tended to be lumped together under the heading of 'witchcraft'. Today, with the existence of mass literacy, the distinction between written and oral traditions has blurred. Thus witchcraft has ceased to be a purely oral phenomenon and now has a considerble body of written magical texts, most of which have emerged in the present century as part of the witchcraft revival. Since witchcraft has a different flavour and character from the Qabalistic-Hermetic type of magic, it is worth treating it separately.

I shall not enter into a discussion of the history of witchcraft and the persecutions that witches have suffered. Nor is this the right place to deal with the vexed questions of what witchcraft really is and whether there is any real continuity between the old pagan cults and the suburban covens of the twentieth century. Let us just say that today there are basically two kinds of witchcraft at work. The first is what is sometimes called 'hereditary'. This is said to be the remnant of the old folk traditions and is practised in rural communities in various parts of Europe. The second kind is the twentieth-century version of witchcraft, based largely on the writings of certain recent apologists for the 'Craft', as its followers call it. Neither kind has anything to do with 'black magic' or 'devil worship'. The emphasis is rather on worship of the deities and forces of nature, notably the great Triple Goddess, associated with the moon, and the Horned God, linked with the sun.

In witchcraft there are no equivalents of the Hermetic writings or the *Key of Solomon*, and it is extremely difficult to find out what the witches of earlier centuries actually did. Most of the documentary evidence consists of grotesquely distorted accounts given in hostile works such as the infamous *Malleus Maleficarum* (Hammer of the Witches), written by two Dominican inquisitors and published in 1486.

It was not until 1899 that there appeared a book purporting to describe objectively the actual conjurations and forms of worship used in witchcraft. This was *Aradia, or the Gospel of the Witches of Italy*. The man responsible for it was an English antiquarian and folklorist named Charles G. Leland. Although his sources were questionable the book became a quarry much used by the architects of the modern witchcraft revival.

The main text of the book is, according to Leland, a translation of a manuscript given to him by an old Italian sorceress named Maddalena. The religion described in it centres around the worship of Diana and her daughter Aradia. 'Diana', writes Leland, 'is set forth ... as the goddess of the god-forsaken and the ungodly, of thieves, harlots and, truthfully enough, of the 'minions of the moon', as Falstaff would have fain had them called.'[1] These people, driven into rebellion by the abuses and injustices of the Church, sought the protection of Diana. The alleged adoration of Satan, says Leland, was a later invention of the Church.

The text of the *Gospel* relates how Diana taught her daughter Aradia 'to work all witchcraft, how to destroy the evil race [of oppressors]'. Aradia then imparted this knowledge to her pupils and said to them:

> When I shall have departed from this world,
> Whenever ye shall have need of anything,
> Once in the month, and when the moon is full,
> Ye shall assemble in some desert place,
> Or in a forest all together join
> To adore the potent spirit of your queen,
> my mother, great Diana ...
> And ye shall all be freed from slavery,

And ye shall be free in everything;
And as the sign that ye are truly free,
Ye shall be naked in your rites, both men
And women also: this shall last until
The last of your oppressors shall be dead ...[2]

Among the ritual formulae included in the text is the 'Conjuration of Diana'. The instructions read as follows:

> You shall make cakes of meal, wine, salt and honey in the shape of a (crescent or horned) moon, and then put them to bake and say:
> I do not bake the bread, nor with it salt,
> Nor do I cook the honey with the wine;
> I bake the body and the blood and soul,
> The soul of (great) *Diana* ...[3]

Besides Leland, two other writers are particularly significant in the modern witchcraft revival. One is Dr Margaret Murray, whose book *The Witch Cult in Western Europe* was published in 1921. Like Leland, she believed that witchcraft was an organized counter-religion based on the worship of Diana. She also held that it involved the periodic ritual sacrifice of a 'Divine King' representing the male deity, and one of her theories was that certain kings of England had been members of the cult. William Rufus, she claimed, had been a 'Divine King' and had willingly submitted himself as a sacrifice.

Margaret Murray's highly questionable theories helped to stimulate interest in the Craft, but it was left to a former colonial officer named Gerald Gardner to supply the real impetus for the witchcraft revival. Gardner was a colourful character who had led a colourful life. Born in England in 1884, he suffered from asthma as a child, and his parents shipped him off in the charge of an Irish nanny on a series of cruises in sunnier climes in the hope of improving his health. Thereafter most of his life was spent outside of Britain. In due course he became a customs officer in Malaya and acquired an expert knowledge of Malayan ceremonial daggers and other curious aspects of Far Eastern folklore. In 1936 he retired from the Colonial

Service and returned to England where he became active in the nudist movement and began to make a name for himself as an eccentric folklorist. In 1939 he joined a witch coven near his home at Christchurch, Hampshire, run by a wealthy woman known as 'Old Dorothy', which claimed to be a continuation of an old rural witchcraft tradition that had survived since pre-Christian times. Gardner felt at home in the Craft and became convinced that he had been a witch in a previous incarnation.

He was not, however, content to remain for long as a mere member of the New Forest coven. In witchcraft he felt he had at last found his true calling. By the end of the war he was in his sixties, and did not want to waste any more time in a subordinate role. In any case he had his own ideas about the kind of witchcraft he wanted to practise. So he travelled to Hastings to see his friend Aleister Crowley, now a frail old gentleman looking more like a retired archdeacon than the Great Beast he had once been. Gardner is said to have commissioned Crowley to write some rituals, which were incorporated into the manual known as the *Book of Shadows*.

For a time Gardner's brand of witchcraft was practised among his own fairly small circle, but in 1949 he published a somewhat turgid novel, *High Magic's Aid,* written under the pseudonym of Scire and dealing with witchcraft in the Middle Ages. This attracted a few new followers. Then, in 1954, appeared his *Witchcraft Today*, an altogether more successful book which stirred up wide interest in the craft. Covens modelling themselves on Gardner's system began to spring up all over the country. In the fifteen years since he had been initiated by 'Old Dorothy', Gardner had succeeded in transforming himself into the Grand Old Man of British Witchcraft.

Meanwhile he had bought a converted windmill and its outbuildings at Castletown, Isle of Man, from Cecil H. Williamson who had founded a witchcraft museum there in the 1940s and later started up a similar museum at Boscastle in Cornwall. Gardner continued the museum, adding to it his vast collection of weapons. He lived there until 1964 when he died on a cruise to the Middle East. His name and the witchcraft system he set in motion have remained very much alive to this day.

Some witch covens continue to guard their writings with secrecy, but in our more tolerant days such precautions are less necessary than they once were, and many witchcraft grimoires have found their way into print.

The *Book of Shadows* has become a general name to refer to any written set of coven rituals, but the particular *Book of Shadows* put together by Crowley and Gardner remains a standard technical manual for the modern Craft. It is a curious blend of Crowley's religion of Thelema, on the one hand, and the Dianic worship recorded by Leland on the other. The tone is well illustrated by the section known as The Charge:

> Listen to the words of the Great Mother who was of old called among men Artemis, Astarte, Diana, Melusine, Ceridwen, Arianrod, Baich and by many other names.
>
> At mine altars the youths of Lacedaemon and Sparta made due sacrifice.
>
> Whenever ye have need of anything, once in the month and better it be if the Moon is full then shall ye assemble in some secret place and adore Me who am Queen of all Witcheries. There shall ye assemble, ye who are fain to learn all sorcery. I shall teach ye things unknown and ye shall be free from all slavery. As a sign that ye be really free ye shall be naked in your rites and ye shall dance, sing, feast, make music, make love — all in Praise of Me. For Mine is the ecstasy of the spirit and Mine is joy on earth, for my Law is Love under Will.
>
> Mine is the secret door of youth, Mine is the Cup of the Wine of Life, Mine is the Cauldron of Ceridwen, Mine is the Holy Grail.
>
> I am the gracious Goddess who gives the gift of joy unto the heart of Man. Upon earth I give unimaginable joys; upon death I give peace, rest and ecstasy. Nor do I demand ought in sacrifice.
>
> Hear ye the words of the Star Goddess, She in the dust of whose feet are the host of Heaven, She whose body encircles the Universe:
>
> I am the Beauty of the Green Earth and the Moon among the Stars, the Mystery of the Waters and the desire in the heart of Man. Arise and come unto Me! From Me all things proceed, unto Me all things return. Before my face ye shall be enfolded in the rapture of the Infinite.

> Let my worship be within the heart that rejoiceth. For all acts of love and pleasure are my rituals ...
>
> Thou who thinkest to seek for Me, know that thy seeking and yearning shall avail thee not unless thou know the Mystery, that if that which thou seekest thou findest not within thee, thou shalt never find it without thee.
>
> For, behold! I have been with thee from the beginning and I am that which is attained at the end of desire.[4]

Most of this invocation is based on Leland's *Aradia*, but it also has stylistic similarities to Crowley's own writings, such as his *Book of Law*.

Numerous witchcraft manuals, mostly stemming from the Gardnerian tradition, have now found their way into print. An example is *Lid off the Cauldron* by a leading British witch, Patricia Crowther (1981). This contains not only an interesting general introduction to witchcraft but also details of many Craft ceremonies and procedures, for example a series of planetary rituals, giving the correspondences of each planet and the invocations to be chanted by the High Priest and Priestess and members of the coven.

In the United States there has been an astonishing proliferation of witchcraft, Gardnerian and otherwise, as is revealed by Margot Adler's remarkable book *Drawing Down the Moon* (1979), subtitled *Witches, Druids, Goddess-Worshippers and Other Pagans in America Today*. An example of an American witchcraft manual is *The Grimoire of Lady Sheba* (1974). The authoress, the book states, 'is a Gardnerian witch, not by Gardnerian initiation, but as an honour extended to her by the Gardnerians. For she has long known of the similarity between her family's *Book of Shadows* and the one kept by the Gardnerians of England, believing that in the far distant past they came from the same source'.[5] The book describes the 'Eightfold Path', a series of techniques and procedures including projection of the astral body, controlled use of drugs, 'the ancient rite of scourging to purify' and 'the great rite' (that is magical sexual union). Details are also given of working tools, recipes for incenses and various spells for different purposes.

In case this summary should mislead the prurient, it

should be emphasized that witchcraft, whether traditional or Gardnerian, is seen by its followers as an idealistic movement which provides a valuable corrective to the patriarchal, mechanistic society in which most of us live.

Turning from the witchcraft revival to modern occultism in general, we find that there are probably more grimoires being printed today than at any other period in history. The present generation of occultists turns hungrily to reprints of the old texts such as the *Key of Solomon* as well as to present-day magical works.

The renewal of the magical tradition in our own era owes a great deal to the Hermetic Order of the Golden Dawn, as I have already shown. But without the texts of the Golden Dawn rituals the order's influence would have been much smaller, and it is thanks to Israel Regardie that these rituals have been made available. In the 1930s Regardie worked his way up through the Stella Matutina branch of the order, then in a state of decay, and decided that the tradition could only be kept alive if the teachings were published. He therefore brought out his four-volume work *The Golden Dawn,* setting out the order's essential teachings. The appearance of the book in 1937–40 aroused much controversy, but it has proved an invaluable manual to the occultists of the post-Second-World-War revival and has been through many editions. Some people might hesitate to call *The Golden Dawn* a grimoire, but, if we define a grimoire as a practical manual of magic, it is no less a grimoire than the *Book of Abra-Melin* or any of the other manuals that have been discussed.

The same is true of Aleister Crowley's classic, *Magick in Theory and Practice,* first published in 1929. A glance at this work will show the remarkable way in which the magical tradition can speak with force to the present. Crowley's magic (or magick, as he spelt it) is based on the injunction 'Do what thou wilt shall be the whole of the Law'. In other words: find the real inner motivating source of your being and act upon it. 'A Man', writes Crowley, 'whose conscious will is at odds with his True Will is wasting his strength.' Such a man he likens to a nation in a state of civil war. Magic can help to unify a person and bring him or her into a true relationship with the universe. Thus Crowley's system is really a form of psychology which, like other psychological systems, aims at bringing the individual into harmony with himself.

In recent years a large number of do-it-yourself books on magic have appeared. One of the better ones is *Techniques of High Magic* by Francis King and Stephen Skinner (1976), a manual based broadly on the Golden Dawn tradition, giving instructions on the making of magical implements, on the performing of rituals and on divination through geomancy and the Tarot.

One of the most interesting twentieth-century writers on magic is the German Franz Bardon, who died in 1958. Bardon was evidently in contact with some powerful central European magical tradition which had developed in a rather different way from the Golden Dawn and similar groups. He was not a figure of colourful notoriety like Crowley, but he has exerted a wide influence through his three main works: *Initiation into Hermetics, The Practice of Magical Evocation* and *The Key to the True Quabbalah*. The first book deals with the development of magical faculties through training in breathing, physical exercises, meditation and visualization and with techniques such as the making of elemental figures. The second book, *The Practice of Magical Evocation* is more like a traditional grimoire. In the first part Bardon gives details of magical techniques, implements and procedures. In the second he describes the hierarchy of spirits and asserts that all the descriptions — several hundred of them — are based on his own contacts with the entities, either by evocations or by mental wandering on the various planes.

Bardon's spirits are classified as follows: there are eight belonging to each of the four elements, 360 belonging to the degrees of the Zodiac and various intelligences belonging to the spheres of the planets. Mercury has seventy-two spirits which bear the names of the angels of the Schemhamphorasch. Bardon, however, says that the name Schemhamphorasch should not be applied to these spirits but only to the unspeakable name of God.

Bardon thus presents a picture of a vast envelope of spiritual energies surrounding the earth, any of which can be contacted by a magician of sufficient skill. In invoking the zodiacal spirits, Bardon works on the basis that each one governs a four-minute period of the twenty-four-hour day, beginning at sunrise. The first four minutes, for example, are governed by Morech, ruler of the 1° Aries, who can 'inform the magician about any questions which are connected with electricity, no matter whether they have to do with electro-technics or with electrophysics, or whether astral or mental electricity, the so-called electric fluid is meant.'

This elaborate hierarchy is reminiscent of the Renaissance memory systems where every branch of human activity had a cosmic pigeon-hole. In Bardon's world we similarly find each intelligence allocated a precise sphere of responsibility. Parmasa (6° Libra) is a master of gaiety, laughter and jokes. Gesegos (7° Libra) governs everything connected with wood. Soteri (8° Libra) has musical instruments as his sphere. Helmis (5° Scorpio) rules everything connected with milk.

The magician who learned how to administer this vast bureaucracy would have some awesome powers at his disposal. But Bardon emphasizes that the whole purpose of magic is self-perfection and that progress can only be made by hard work and training. His system is certainly not one to embark upon casually, but like all magical systems it imposes a discipline that would inevitably transform whoever worked with it.

16.
Grimoires in Literature

Such is the fascination exerted by the very idea of a book of occult secrets that the image of such a book has itself become an archetype. This can be seen in the many works of literature where grimoires play an important role.

One such work is the novel *The Column of Dust* (1909) by Evelyn Underhill, a member of A.E. Waite's branch of the Golden Dawn. The heroine, Constance Tyrrel, is a bookseller's assistant who decides, out of curiosity and lust for adventure, to try an evocation from the *Grand Grimoire*. The novel opens with her performing the ritual in the deserted bookshop by candlelight, standing inside a charcoal circle with the grimoire lying open on a desk beside her, 'a stained and coarsely printed duodecimo'. As she chants the words of power a small column of dust rises from the floor and a pitiful voice cries: 'Ah, what has happened? I am caught! I cannot get away!'[1] She has drawn a spirit entity into the confines of matter. Henceforth the 'Watcher', as this entity is called, haunts her constantly. At first he is a being without love, aims or values, but gradually he develops more human qualities. In the end Constance pays for her folly by having to sacrifice her own life, but what she has done has not been entirely in vain, for the Watcher finally becomes a true human soul.

A similar incautious evocation is the subject of a short story entitled *The Grimoire* [2] by Montague Summers, a Catholic priest best known for his books on the history of witchcraft and magic, written from an almost Inquisitorial point of view and deeply hostile to the occult. Summers was, however, a not unengaging figure and was for a time friendly with Aleister Crowley. His story concerns one Dr Julian Hodsoll, a collector of occult books who one day enters a bookshop where he is a regular customer and asks the dealer, Merritt, if there is anything in his line in the shop that day. Merritt tells him that he has acquired something the day before, and hands him 'a podgy octavo vellum volume' entitled *Mysterium Arcanum, seu de daemonibus rite evocandis cum quibisdam aliis secretis abditissimis* (The Secret Mystery, or the Art of Evoking Evil Spirits with certain other most curious and close matters). It is marked 'Romae, sine permissu superiorum' (printed at Rome without the permission of the authorities). Hodsoll buys the book and takes it with him when he goes to stay in the country with his friend Canon Spenlow, a fellow bibliophile. When shown the volume the Canon is shocked and advises him to burn it. Hodsoll refuses to do this and instead settles down in his bedroom to examine the book. He copies out a hand-written evocation which he finds at the back of the volume and, in order to check it, repeats it softly to himself. Immediately there comes a light tap at the door. The narrative continues:

> 'You wanted me, sir', said a low voice.
>
> Dr Hodsoll turned and saw that there had entered the room and was standing waiting his orders a tall young man with the impassive features and formal bearing of a well-trained servant. He was dressed not in livery, but in a smartly-cut black suit, and seemed the very pattern of a gentleman's valet. At the same time there was something in his appearance, which was perhaps due to his large dark eyes, full of infinite sadness and a yearning regret, and the extreme pallor of his countenance.

This sinister figure, whom we are to assume is the Devil, plagues Hodsoll with his increasingly malevolent presence until a Dominican friar, Father Raphael Grant, who is staying at the house as a guest, comes to the rescue. In his bedroom one night Hodsoll, paralysed with terror, is about to be attacked by the fiend, when the Dominican enters the room and carries out a ritual of exorcism. The shaken Hodsoll ends by being converted and entering the order himself.

An even more chilling atmosphere pervades the works of the American writer H.P. Lovecraft (1890–1937), a master of the genre of the horror story. In Lovecraft's work the invisible world of strange, dormant gods is always ready to burst forth alarmingly into the peaceful New England environment which most of his characters inhabit. Readers of his stories gradually become acquainted with a whole mythology, full of weird and curiously evocative names. This mythology contains two sets of gods: the benevolent 'Elder Gods', about whom very little is said; and the far from benevolent 'Ancient Ones' or 'Great Old Ones'. Chief among the latter is Cthulhu, who is described as a hideous sea monster, dwelling in the Great Deep, a sort of primeval ocean. There are also Azathoth and Yog Sothoth, the two gods of chaos, Shub Niggurath, the 'goat with a thousand young', and others with similarly barbaric-sounding names.

Many of the stories mention a book used for the evocation of these beings, which is entitled the *Necronomicon* (the 'Book of Dead Names'). In a letter to Clark Ashton Smith in 1927, Lovecraft described the impressive provenance that he had worked out for this book.[3] It was written, he says, by the mad Arab, Abdul Alhazred, a native of Sanáa in Yemen, who flourished in about AD 700 and learnt the worship of Yog Sothoth and Cthulhu while visiting the devil-haunted wastes of the southern Arabian deserts. The book, originally entitled *Al Azif,* was a product of his old age. In AD 950 it was translated into Greek and given the title *Necronomicon*. A century later it was burnt at the order of Michael, Patriarch of Constantinople. It was translated into Latin by one Olaus in 1228, but placed on the Index by Pope Gregory IX in 1232. The orginal Arabic was lost before Olaus's time, and the last known Greek copy was destroyed in Salem in 1692. The book was printed in the fifteenth, sixteenth and seventeenth centuries, but few copies are extant. 'Wherever existing,' Lovecraft states, 'it is carefully guarded for the sake of the world's welfare and sanity.'

So powerful is the mythology created by Lovecraft that many people are convinced that he was, consciously or unconsciously, in possession of real occult knowledge.

Kenneth Grant, for example, in his book *The Magical Revival,* points out the parallels between Lovecraft's images and the symbols used by the Golden Dawn and Aleister Crowley. Grant sees the *Necronomicon* as corresponding to Crowley's *Book of Law.*

Not only has Lovecraft been credited with esoteric knowledge, but it has been claimed that he based his *Necronomicon* on a real book. This idea has stimulated Lovecraft's admirers to much research in pursuit of the orginal work and has led to the publication of at least six spoof *Necronomicons.* One of these was published under the title of *Al Azif* with an introduction by L. Sprague de Camp. Another was put together by George Hay, Robert Turner and David Langford and published as the *Necronomicon,* with an introduction by Colin Wilson.[4] This version purports to be a deciphering of John Dee's *Liber Logaeth.* It is, however, clear from the text that the whole affair is not to be taken seriously, as the following quotation shows:

> In ye North beyond the stone of Great Coldness set ye first ye stone of Saturn at space of three paces. This being done proceed thou widdershins placing at like distances apart ye stones of Jupiter, Mercury, Mars, Venus, Sol and Luna ...
>
> At ye centre of the so completed configuration set ye the Altar of ye Great Old Ones and seal it with ye symbol of Yog-Sothoth and ye mighty names of Azathoth, Cthulhu, Hastur, Shub-Niggurath and Nyarlathotep.
>
> And ye stones shall be ye Gates through which thou shalt call them forth from Outside man's time and space.

Yet another version of the *Necronomicon* was published in New York in 1977, a lavish production in a silver-embossed black binding, illustrated with many sigils and containing some impressive-sounding invocations.[5] Here, for example, is the 'Invocation of the Eastern Gate':

> Thee I invoke, Mistress of the Rising Star,
> Queen of Magick, of the Mountains of MASHU!
> Thee I call forth to guard this Most Holy mandal against the
> Seven Ensnarers,, the Seven Liers-In-Wait, the evil
> Maskim, the Evil Lords!

> Thee I summon, Queen of the Eastern Ways, that thou
> mayest protect me from the Eye of Death, and the
> evil rays of the ENDUKUGGA and NINDUKUGGA!
> Be watchful, Queen of the Eastern Ways, and Remember!
> Spirit of the East, Remember!

The introduction to this book states: 'In the interim period between the translation and publication of this work, the Editor, along with a circle of initiates in another discipline, undertook to experiment with the rituals and forces outlined in the NECRONOMICON.' They came to the alarming conclusion that *'there are no effective banishings for the forces invoked in the NECRONOMICON itself* !' They do add, however, that solar formulae such as the Jewish Kaddish prayer and the Lord's Prayer are helpful, since the *Necronomicon*, with its allegedly Sumerian roots, is lunar in nature.

Stories about grimoires and imaginative hoaxes like the *Necronomicon* forgeries are characteristic of the strange stratum between reality and fantasy that so many occultists occupy. This stratum is perhaps closer to the surface of everyday life than many of us realize, and it is continually poking through. Literature is only one way in which it does so. It is also felt in the visual arts and in music, but these we cannot enter into here in any detail, since this is primarily a book about books.

17.
Talking of the Devil

The books on the Devil's shelf have so far proved, for the most part, to have very little to do with the Devil himself, but the time has now come to give him his due. How does Satan fit into the picture? And what part does the worship of evil play in this story?

The answer to the second question is: very little. Most people who have been accused of 'black magic' have not been devotees of evil but merely practitioners of a form of magic which the Church found dangerous or heretical. A moment's reflection will show that to worship the principle of evil is an illogicality. Every act that a person commits is carried out because it seems good at the time to the person responsible, however evil it might seem to others. Therefore someone who committed himself to a life of evil would merely be setting up evil as his own good. But this would involve him in a continual dilemma. He must always do the opposite of good, but as soon as he has set up the opposite, that becomes good and he must discard it. Thus, those who profess to worship Satan are not really devoting themselves to an abstract principle of evil, but are rather poking their tongues out at Christianity and Christian values.

Even this form of Satanism was not nearly as widespread as the Church inquisitors maintained. No doubt there were a few out-and-out Satanists and some who were led into evil forms of magic through greed or ignorance. I do not propose here to enter into the stories of Urbain Grandier, Gilles de Rais and La Voisin. They can be read about in the numerous histories of magic and witchcraft that are available today. These individuals may or may not have practised distasteful forms of magic, but it is doubtful whether they were Satanists in any meaningful sense of the word.

As for the notion of a pact with the Devil, this can be traced back to the writings of certain of the early Church fathers, chiefly Augustine who, in his *de Doctrina Christiana*, condemned all occult arts as 'arising from the pestiferous association of men with demons, as if formed by a pact of faithless and dishonourable friendship'. The scriptural reference used to support this idea was Isaiah 28, 15, which was misleadingly translated in the Vulgate to suggest the possibility of a contract with the Devil: 'We have signed a treaty with death and with hell we have made a pact.' By the sixth century stories had begun to circulate about people who had made such pacts. A well-known example was the story of Theophilus, a Christian who signed a parchment renouncing Christ and the Virgin in return for help from the powers of hell in reinstating him as steward of his local church after rivals had succeeded in having him dismissed. Subsequently, in remorse, he prayed to the Virgin, and she appeared and returned the parchment to him.

Many forms of pact with the demonic powers are described in the grimoires, but most of the texts dealing with such pacts advise the magician either to refuse to surrender his soul or to pretend to agree but leave some loophole enabling him to renege on the pact. The famous pact with Lucifer allegedly signed by Urbain Grandier and used in evidence at his trial in 1634 was undoubtedly a forgery planted by his enemies.

The spectre of Satanism might have declined into an innocuous old age as scepticism advanced and Christianity retreated. But in the nineteenth century it caught the imagination of an age that was already revolting against rationalism. In France particularly Satanism became a popular topic. The way in which it titillated the artists of the Symbolist movement is illustrated in a drawing by Félicien Rops, *la Lecture de Grand Albert* (Fig. 10), showing a naked woman with a delicate pair of horns and a broomstick between her legs, reading a huge grimoire propped up on a table under which a sinister monkey is squatting.

One of the defenders of Satanism was the French historian Jules Michelet, who argued in his book *La Sorcière* that medieval sorcery was a movement towards liberation from narrow religious dogma. Its practitioners, he says, were mainly women, because the female sex could not express its true nature through Christianity. Thus the black mass, he argues, can be interpreted as a 'redemption of Eve'. A different view was taken by Jules Bois whose book *Le Satanisme et la magie* presents Satanism as a fiendish conspiracy. But possibly the most interesting account of Satanism at this period is given in J.-K. Huysmans' novel, *Là-Bas* (1891), which includes a full description of a black mass. Huysmans' friend the Abbé Boullan, from whom he obtained much of the information for *Là-Bas,* had a reputation as an arch-Satanist, but it is difficult to find much hard and fast evidence of genuine Satanism at that period.

For this we have to wait until the twentieth century. At the present time the best known Satanist movement is the Church of Satan, based in California and led by Anton Szandor LaVey. The doctrines and rites of this church are described in LaVey's two books *The Satanic Bible* and *The Satanic Rituals*. LaVey is at pains to make it clear that he does not accept the Christian evaluation of Satan as an evil being. The Satan that LaVey and his followers worship is a primordial force cognate with Pan, who serves as a focus for a general spirit of rebellion and iconoclasm. LaVey is aware of the dilemmas inherent in Satan worship. 'It will be observed', he writes in *The Satanic Rituals,* 'that a pervasive element of paradox runs throughout the rituals contained herein. Up is down, pleasure is pain, darkness is light, slavery is freedom, madness is sanity, etc. ... This is not intended solely to serve as blasphemy — on the contrary, it is used to make it apparent that things are not always as they seem and that *no* standard can or should be deified, for under the proper conditions any standard can be changed.' As for the Black Mass, LaVey declares that 'it is usually entered into for a personal need to purge oneself, via over-compensation, for inhibiting guilts imposed by Christian dogma'.[1]

The rituals contained in the book are a curious selection.

There is a French Black Mass, a German rite called *Das Tierdrama* (the Animal Drama) and another German ceremony called *Die elektrischen Vorspiele* (the Electric Preludes), a neo-pagan ritual which allegedly found its way into the liturgy of the Nazi SS. There is also a rite called the Ceremony of the Nine Angels, using a strange, Lovecraftian language to invoke the 'Old Ones' of H.P. Lovecraft's Cthulhu mythos. It is all very colourful, and just wicked enough to *épater les bourgeois*.

Other versions of Satanism surface periodically in different parts of the world. Sometimes they are real attempts to establish a form of worship opposing everything that Christianity stands for. But what the public hears about more often, through the popular press and pulp literature on the subject, are the amateurish cases of the 'Clapham black magic sex orgy' variety. Many people still tend to put magic of any kind into the Satanic category. I have included the present chapter to correct this impression and to emphasize that Satanism has a relatively small place in the history of magical literature.

Having surveyed that history from ancient Egyptian times up to the present day, we are left wondering what lessons are to be learnt from it. Were the writers of the *Key of Solomon, The Sixth and Seventh Books of Moses, the Sworn Book of Honorius* and all the other grimoires merely wasting their time? To answer that we must also ask whether magic itself has any value.

Magic and mysticism are both ways of contacting the divine world. The essential difference between the two is that the mystic tries to raise his consciousness out of the mundane sphere through meditation and contemplation. The magician, on the other hand, draws power down into the world and actively uses it. The latter is a dangerous procedure, and many magicians have been destroyed by it. Others have wasted their time dabbling in spells and incantations to no effect. Yet in a few cases, such as the two I quoted in my chapter on the Abra-Melin system, the practice of magic has brought about a genuine and positive spiritual tranformation.

It is true that magic is about power and that power is dangerous. But have the magicians been any less responsible in their use of power than the priests of modern science? The late Jack Parsons, an American physicist of genius and also a magician of the Crowleyan school, wrote in an eloquent little essay on witchcraft of the 'demons in the shape of monstrous machines' that rule the nightmares of modern man. The point he was making was that the demons conjured up by science are far more terrifying than anything conjured up by the sorcerers. Since we cannot shut away the powers that have been unleashed on the world we must surely learn to control them in a spirit of humility and reverence. Perhaps the few magicians who have succeeded in doing this have an important lesson to teach us. If so, the grimoires will not have been written in vain.

1. Frontispiece to a 1502 edition of *The Book of Secrets* by Albertus Magnus. The great Dominican scholar is shown studying while his students take notes. Probably it was one such student who wrote down the *Book of Secrets*.

2. Paracelsus (1493–1541), author of many works on alchemy and related subjects. One of the books attributed to him, the *Archidoxis Magica*, a sort of medical grimoire, is probably spurious.

3. A sixteenth-century German engraving of a sorcerer at work, armed with grimoire and magic sword and standing within a circle of protection. (Warburg Institute).

4. *The Dance of the Witches,* an engraving from a painting by Jacob de Gheyn (1565–1629). The witch seated in the centre foreground has a large grimoire lying open in front of her. (Warburg Institute).

5. An etching by Rembrandt showing the scene in Goethe's play where Faust contemplates the sign of the macrocosm.

6. Two magicians, alleged to be John Dee and Edward Kelley, raising a ghost in the churchyard at Walton-le-Dale, Lancashire, with the help of a book of conjurations. The identification of the figures as Dee and Kelley is questionable.

7. The magician shown in a positive light. Kneeling in front of an altar supporting two grimoires, he receives angelic wisdom from above, while demons are kept at bay by his magic circle. The illustration forms the frontispiece to *The Astrologer in the Nineteenth Century* (1825).

8. (a) The spirit Oberion, appearing as a sçaly monster with the face of a woman, and (b) the circle for raising Oberion: two illustrations from *The Astrologer in the Nineteenth Century*.

9. Three talismans illustrated in *The Astrologer in the Nineteenth Century*. They are, from top to bottom, for use against enemies, for war and battle and for love.

10. *La lecture de Grand Albert:* a drawing by the nineteenth-century Belgian artist, Félicien Rops.

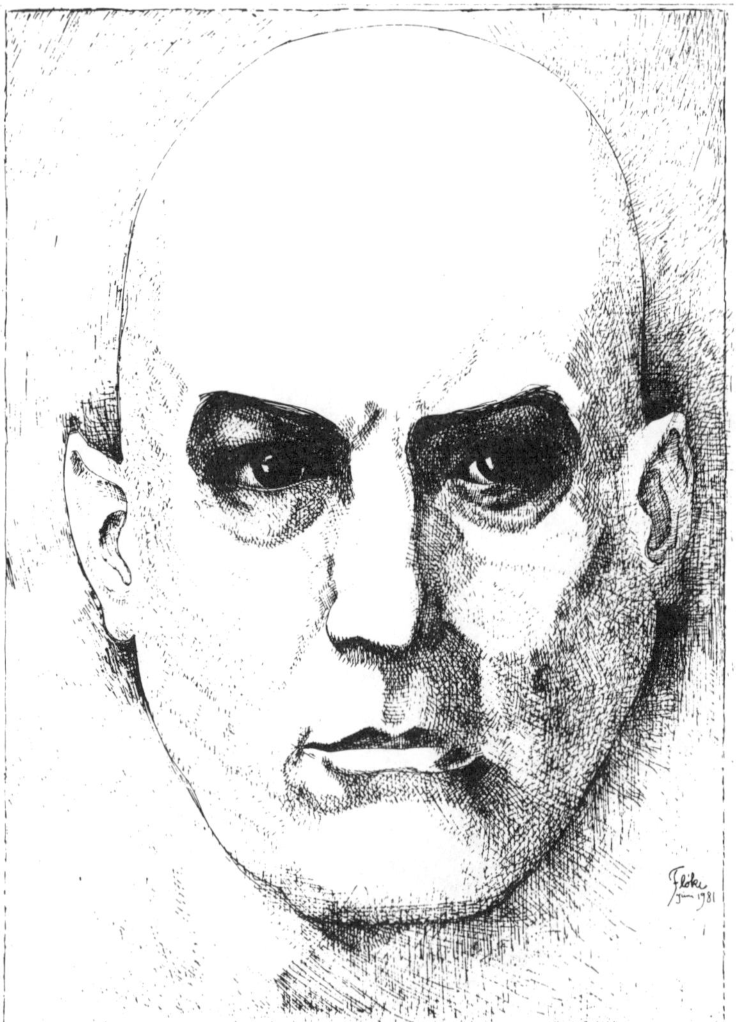

11. Aleister Crowley: a portrait drawn in 1981 by the Icelandic artist Alfred Floki. Crowley's *Magick in Theory and Practice* is one of the classic twentieth-century manuals of magic.

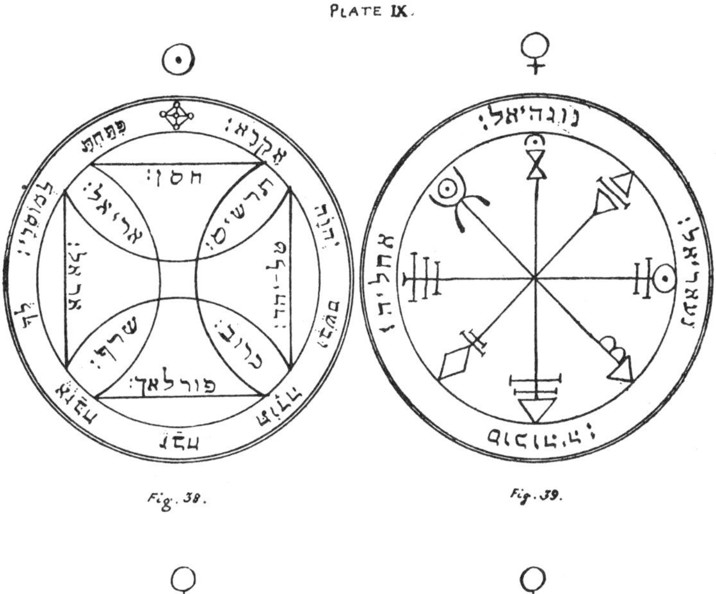

12. Pentacles of the Sun and Venus from S.L. MacGregor Mathers' edition of *The Key of Solomon*.

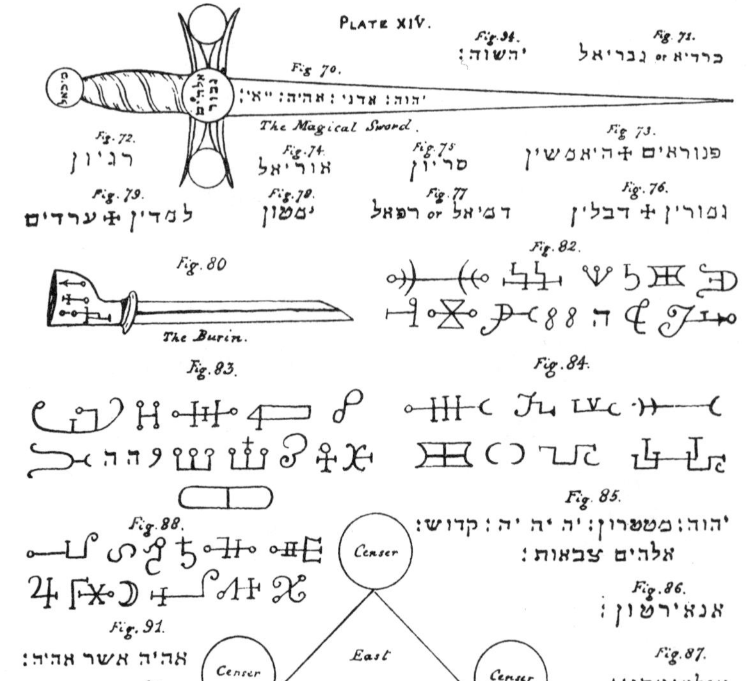

13. A page of illustrations from the Mathers edition of *The Key of Solomon,* showing the magical sword and burin, various formulae to be inscribed on the magician's equipment, and the layout of the circle used in his operations.

Part II

EXTRACTS FROM THE GRIMOIRES

18.
A Magical Papyrus

One of the most interesting of the magical papyri to have come down to us from the religious melting pot of Hellenistic Egypt is a text found at Thebes, dating from the third century AD and written in Egyptian demotic script. Like the *Picatrix,* this document is an example of how such magical works seem to have the power to survive against the odds. It was discovered in the early part of the nineteenth century and bought by the Swedish consul at Alexandria. Somehow the papyrus became separated into two halves, one of which ended up in the Leiden Museum of Antiquities and the other in the British Museum. Not until the 1890s was the connection between the two halves spotted by Dr Pleyte of the Leiden Museum. An English version, from which the following quotations are taken, was edited by F.L. Griffith and Herbert Thompson (London. H. Grevel & Co., 1904).

The text is broadly Gnostic in character and consists of a compilation of spells, invocations and magical remedies. It is a good example of the period of transition from the exalted magic of ancient Egypt to the lower magic of the grimoires. Much of the language is of great beauty, as these extracts show. The first is a divination procedure using a boy as a medium. The second is a formula for making a love potion.

An Inquiry of the Lamp

You go to a clean dark cell without light and you dig a new hole in an east wall and you take a white lamp in which no minium or gum water has been put, its wick being clean, and you fill it with clean genuine Oasis oil, and you recite the spells of praising Ra at dawn in his rising and you bring the lamp when lighted opposite the sun and recite to it the spells as below four times, and you take it into the cell, you being pure, and the boy also, and you pronounce the spells to the boy, he not looking at the lamp, his eyes being closed, seven times. You put pure frankincense on the brazier. You put your finger on the boy's head, his eyes being closed. When you have finished you make him open his eyes towards the lamp; then he sees the shadow of the god about the lamp, and he inquires for you concerning that which you desire. You must do it at midday in a place without light. If it be that you are inquiring for a spirit damned, a wick of sail-cloth(?) is what you put in the lamp and you fill it with clean butter. If it is some other business, a clean wick with pure genuine oil is that which you put in the lamp; if you will do it to bring a woman to a man, ointment of roses is that which you put in the lamp. You must lay the lamp on a new brick and the boy also must sit on another brick with his eyes closed. You cry down into his head four times.

The spells which you recite (to the lamp) to the wick previously before you recite to the boy: formula: 'Art thou the unique great wick of the linen of Thoth? Art thou the byssus robe of Osiris, the divine Drowned, woven by the hand of Isis, spun by the hand of Nephthys? Art thou the original band that was made for Osiris Khentamente? Art thou the great bandage with which Anubis put forth his hand to the body of Osiris the mighty god? I have brought thee to-day—ho! thou wick—to cause the boy to look into thee, that thou mayest make reply to every matter concerning which I ask here today. Is it that you will (?) not do it? O wick, I have put thee in the hand of the black cow, I have lighted thee in the hand of the female cow. Blood of the Drowned one is that which I put to thee for oil; the hand of Anubis is that which is laid on thee. The spells of the great Sorcerer are those which I recite to thee. Do thou bring me the god in whose hand is the command today and let him give me answer as to everything about which I inquire here today truly without falsehood. Ho! Nut, mother of water, ho! Apet, mother of fire, come unto me, Nut, mother of water, come Apet, mother of fire, come unto me Yaho'. You say it drawling (?) with your voice exceedingly. You say again: Esex, Poe, Ef-khe-ton,' otherwise said, 'Khet-on,' seven times. If it is a direct (?) inquiry, these alone are the things that you recite to the lamp, and you lie down without speaking. But if obduracy take place, you rise, you recite his summons, which is his compulsion. Formula: 'I am the Ram's face, Youth is my name; I was born under the venerable persea in Abydos, I am the soul of the great chief who is in Abydos; I am the guardian of the great corpse that is in U-pek; I am he whose eyes are as the eyes of Akhom when he watcheth Osiris by night; I am Teptuf upon the desert of Abydos; I am he that watcheth the great corpse which is in Busiris; I am he who watcheth for Light-scarab-noble (?).' The spells that you write on the lamp, Bakhukhsikhukh 'whose name is hidden in my heart; Bibiou (Soul of souls) is his name.' Formula, seven times. If it is a direct (?) inquiry, these things alone are what you recite. If it is an inquiry by the boy that you are about, you recite these aforesaid to the lamp before calling down into the head of the boy, you turn round (?), you recite this other invocation to the lamp also. Formula: 'O Osiris, O lamp that giveth vision of the things [of days] above, that giveth vision of the things below and vice versa; O lamp (*bis*), Amen is moored in thee; O lamp (*bis*) I invoke thee, thou goest up to the shore of the great sea, the sea of Syria, the sea of Osiris. Do I speak to thee? Dost thou come that I may send thee? Ho, lamp witness (?) to thyself, since thou hast found Osiris upon his boat of papyrus and *teḥen*, Isis being at his head, Nephthys at his feet, and the male and female gods about him. Speak, Isis, let it be told to Osiris concerning the things which I ask about, to cause the god to come in whose hand is the command, and give me answer to everything about which I shall inquire here today. When Isis said 'Let a god be summoned to me that I may send him, he being discreet (?) as to the business on which he will go and he accomplish it,' they went and they brought to her; thou art the lamp that was brought to her. The fury of Sekhmet thy mother and of Heke thy father is cast at thee, thou shalt not be lighted for Osiris and Isis, thou shalt not be lighted for Anubis until thou hast given me an answer to everything which I ask about here today truly without telling me falsehood. If thou wilt not do it, I will not give thee oil.

A Potion

You take a little shaving of the head of a man who has died a violent death, together with seven grains of barley that has been buried in a grave of a dead (?) man; you pound them with ten *oipe*, otherwise nine, (of) apple-seeds (?); you add blood of a worm (?) of a black dog to them, with a little blood of your second finger, (that) of the heart (?), of your left hand, and with your semen (?), and you pound them together and put them into a cup of wine and add three *uteh* to it of the first-fruits of the vintage, before you have tasted it and before they have poured out from it; and you pronounce this invocation to it seven times and you make the woman drink it; and you tie the skin of the parasite aforesaid with a band of byssus and tie it to your left arm. Its invocation, formula: 'I am he of Abydos in truth, by formation (?) (and?) birth in her (?) name of Isis the bringer (?) of fire, she of the mercy-seat of the Agathodaemon. I am this figure of the sun, *Sitamesro* is my name I am this figure of a Captain of the host, very valiant, this Sword (?), this Overthrower (?), the Great Flame is my name. I am this figure of Horus, this Fortress (?), this Sword (?), this Overthrower (?) is my name. I am this figure of One Drowned, that testifieth by writing, that resteth on the other side (?) here under the great offering-table (?) of Abydos; as to which the blood of Osiris bore witness to her (?) name of Isis when it (the blood) was poured into this cup, this wine. Give it, blood of Osiris (that?) he (?) gave to Isis to make her feel love in her heart for him night and day at any time, there not being time of deficiency. Give it, the blood of N. born of N. to give it to N. born of N. in this cup, this bowl of wine today, to cause her to feel a love for him in her heart, the love that Isis felt for Osiris, when she was seeking after him everywhere, let N. the daughter of N. feel it, she seeking after N. the son of N. everywhere; the longing that Isis felt for Horus of Edfu, let N. born of N. feel it, she loving him, mad after him, inflamed by him, seeking him everywhere, there being a flame of fire in her heart in her moment of not seeing him.'

19.
TIBETAN MAGIC

A comparison was made in Chapter 4 between the circles used by western magicians and the mandalas of Hinduism and Buddhism. This is only one of the many parallels between occidental and oriental occult systems. The similarities are particularly striking in the case of Tibetan Buddhism with its complex ritual practices, many of them based on pre-Buddhist shamanism. René de Nebesky-Wojkowitz, in his remarkable study *Oracles and Demons of Tibet*, gives a detailed account of Tibetan magic, which reveals a world very similar to that of the western grimoires.

As in western occultism, there is a huge bureaucracy of demons, each with its attributes, responsibilities and sphere of action. In conjuring such demons it is important to observe the correct correspondences: points of the compass, colours, symbols and so on. One healing ritual, for example, involves setting up a kind of altar on which is placed a drawing of an eight-petalled lotus. The central section of the lotus is coloured white, the eastern one is sky blue, the southern yellow, the western red and the northern green. In the centre is set a vessel containing a clay effigy of the sick person, wrapped in a piece of cloth whose colour must correspond to the element attributed to the year in which the person was born. Around the altar are a series of concentric circles, made up of lamps, sacrificial cakes and other ritual objects. During the ceremony, various deities belonging to the quarters are invoked.

The 'black' magical formulae of Tibet show even more striking similarities with their western counterparts, as is clear from the following description of part of a ritual for killing an enemy:

> First some nail clippings or a piece of a worn dress have to be procured surreptitiously from the potential victim or, if none of these things can be obtained, at least some earth from his footprints should be taken. A circle is drawn on a piece of paper and then divided by two lines into four equal sections. In the centre of the circle is outlined the image of the man or woman — representing the victim — its hands and feet bound by heavy chains. All around this figure various curses are written in a circle ... Then a few drops of the menstruation blood of a prostitute are smeared on each curse, the hair, nails etc. of the victim are placed on the figure previously drawn, and the paper is folded up and wrapped in a piece of cloth soiled by a prostitute's monthly flow. The package is now placed in the right horn of a wild yak and the following things are added: a small quantity of blood from a man, a woman, a goat and a dog, some earth from a crossroad, iron and brass filings which have been obtained from a blacksmith, a piece of rope — or a piece of some other object — by means of which somebody has committed suicide, the bone, skin or hair of a woman who died in childbirth, some aconite, a piece of the underwear of a widow, and some water from a subterranean spring ...[1]

Another Tibetan source worth quoting is the *Hevajra Tantra*, a manual of ritual centering on the divinity Hevajra (meaning 'final truth') and his consort Nairātmyā. Like many of its western counterparts, it is a curious mixture of lofty religious sentiment and practical magic. Here, for example, is a rain-producing ritual:

> OṂ ĀḤ PHUḤ. Intoning these syllables, make an image of a snake, wash it with the five ambrosias [the five products of the cow], honour it with lotuses, smear it with nāga-subduing juice [*nāga* is the word for snake], smear its head with ichor, and having made a pot by placing two dishes together, lay the snake inside. Then fill the pot with milk from a black cow and wrap it in a woven cloth that has been cut by a dark-skinned girl. Then in the north-west make a small pool, and place the snake in it. At its edge lay out the *maṇḍala*. Black colouring is obtained from charcoal of the cemetery, white from ground human bones, yellow from

green lac, red from cemetery-bricks, green from *caurya* leaves and ground human bones, and dark blue from ground human bones and cemetery charcoal. With these colours lay out the *maṇḍala*, measuring it with a cemetery thread [i.e., made from the guts of a corpse] three cubits, three inches in size. In the centre draw Hevajra in the act of trampling on a snake; he has eight faces, four feet, sixteen arms and twenty-four eyes. Then the master, his mind resolved in imost wrath, should utter this *mantra* in that lonely spot:

> OM GHURU GHURU GHUDU GHUDU GHATA GHATA GHOTAYA GHOTAYA
> O Lord of the *nagas* who causes snakes to tremble, He-he Ru-ru Ka — those *nagas* who have gone to the seven lower realms, drag them forth, drag them forth, rain, rain, thunder, thunder — PHUḤ PHUḤ PHUḤ PHUḤ PHUḤ PHUḤ PHUḤ PHUḤ HUṂ HUṂ HUṂ PHAṬ SVĀHĀ.

If it does not produce rain now, one should recite this *mantra* backwards.[2]

20.
The Book of Secrets of Albertus Magnus

As already mentioned, Albertus Magnus was revered as one of the great philosopher-magicians of the Middle Ages. The *Book of Secrets* attributed to him belongs in the category of natural rather than demonic magic and is a good example of the way in which science and magic at that period were inseparably connected. In the section quoted here the author gives recipes for using precious stones to bring about marvellous effects. The text is from the English version published in about 1550. It is most conveniently available in the edition of Michael R. Best and Frank H. Brightman (Oxford, Clarendon Press, 1973).

Of the Virtues of Certain Stones

If thou wilt know whether thy wife be chaste, or no.

Take the stone which is called *Magnes,* in English the Loadstone. It is of sad blue colour, and it is found in the sea of India, sometimes in parts of Almany, in the province which is called East France. Lay this stone under the head of a wife, and if she be chaste, she will embrace her husband; if she be not chaste, she will fall anon forth of the bed. Moreover, if this stone be put brayed and scattered upon coals, in four corners of the house, they that be sleeping shall flee the house, and leave all.

If thou wilt be made invisible.

Take the stone which is called *Ophthalmus,* and wrap it in the leaf of the Laurel, or Bay tree; and it is called *Lapis*

Obtalmicus, whose colour is not named, for it is of many colours. And it is of such virtue, that it blindeth the sights of them that stand about. Constantius carrying this in his hand, was made invisible by it.

If thou wilt provoke sorrow, fear, terrible fantasies, and debate.

Take the stone which is called *Onyx*, which is of black colour. And the kind is best which is full of white veins. And it cometh from India, unto Araby, and if it be hanged upon the neck, or finger, it stirreth up anon sorrow or heaviness in a man, and terrors, and also debate. And this hath been proved by men of late time.

If thou wilt burn any man's hands without fire.

Take the stone which is called *Peridonius*, which is of yellow colour, which if it be hanged upon the neck of any man, it healeth *Areticum*. And also if this stone be gripped straitly, it burneth the hand anon, and therefore it must be touched lightly, and gently.

If thou wilt kindle the mind of any man to joys, and make his wit sharp.

Take the stone which is called *Selenites*. It groweth in the bosom of a snail of India, called Tortoise, and there is of divers kinds of it, of white, red, and purple colour. Others say that it is green, and found in the parts of Persia. And also old Philosophers say, if it be tasted, it giveth knowledge of certain things to come. If it be put under the tongue, specially in the first [day of the] Moon, it hath a virtue only for an hour. Therefore being in the tenth day of the Moon, it hath this virtue in the first or tenth hour. The method of divination is this: when it is under the tongue, if our thought be of any business, whether it ought to be or no, if it ought to be, it is fixed steadfastly to the heart, so that it may not be plucked away, if not, the heart leapeth aback from it. Also Philosophers have said that it healeth phthisics, and weak men.

If thou wilt that seething water come forth anon, after thou hast put in thy hand.

Take the stone which is called *Topazos* from the isle

Topazis, or because it showeth a similitude of gold. And there be two kinds of it; one is utterly like gold and this is more precious, the other kind is of the colour of saffron, of brighter colour than gold is, and this is more profitable. It hath been proved, in our time, that if it be put in seething water it maketh it to run over, but if thou put thy hand in it, the water is drawn out anon, and one of our brethren did this at Paris. It is good also against *emothoicam et stimaticam*, or lunatic passion or grief.

If thou wilt pluck off the skin of thine, or another man's hand.

Take the stone which is called *Medius*, of the region Media, in the which the people dwelling are called Medes. And there be two kinds of it, black and green. It is said of old Philosophers and also of Philosophers being in this time, if the black be broken, and resolved in hot water, if any man wash his hands in that water, the skin of his hands shall be plucked off anon. Philosophers say also, that it is good against the gout, and blindness of the eyes, and it nourisheth hurt and weak eyes.

If thou wilt that a man suffer no pain, nor be tormented.

Take the stone which is called *Memphites*, of the city which is called Memphis, and it is a stone of such virtue as Aaron and Hermes say: if it be broken, and mixed with water, and given to him to drink, which should be burned, or suffer any torments, that drink induceth so great unableness to feel, that he that suffereth, feeleth neither pain nor tormenting.

If thou wilt make a fire continually unable to be quenched or put out.

Take the stone which is called *Asbestos*, and it is of the colour of Iron, and there is found very much of it in Arabia. If that stone be kindled or inflamed, it may never be put out, or quenched, because it hath the nature of the first feathers of the Salamander, by reason of moisty fatness, which nourisheth the fire kindled in it.

If thou wilt overcome thy enemies.

Take the stone which is called *Adamas*, in English speech a Diamond, and it is of shining colour, and very hard, in so much that it cannot be broken, but by the blood of a Goat, and it groweth in Arabia, or in Cyprus. And if it be bounden to the left side, it is good against enemies, madness, wild beasts, venomous beasts, and cruel men, and against chiding and brawling, and against venom, and invasion of fantasies. And some call it *Diamas*.

21.
THE LEMEGETON

The *Lemegeton,* or *Lesser Key of Solomon the King,* is a work of pure demonic magic and was regarded as one of the most authoritative of the grimoires during the seventeenth and eighteenth centuries, though the full text never appeared in printed form. It exists in two English manuscripts in the British Library (Sloane 2731 and 3648), the first of which was begun in 1676. The following list of the seventy-two spirits, given in the *Lemegeton* along with their sigils, is taken from A.E.Waite's *Book of Black Magic*. The spirits are also listed in Idries Shah's book *The Secret Lore of Magic*.

The Mysteries of Goëtic Theurgy according to the Lesser Key of Solomon the King

I.—Concerning the Spirits of the Brazen Vessel, otherwise called the False Monarchy of Demons.

The Goëtic Art of Solomon gives instructions for the evocation of the seventy-two spirits whom the King of Israel, according to a well-known legend, shut up in a brass vessel and cast into a deep lake. When the vessel was discovered by the Babylonians, it was supposed to contain a great treasure, and was accordingly broken open. The spirits who were thus set at liberty, together with their legions, returned to their former places, Belial excepted, who entered into a certain image, and gave oracles to the people of the country in return for sacrifices and divine honours. Their names and offices are as follows:

I. BAAL, a king ruling in the East, who imparts invisibility and wisdom. He appears with a human head, or with that of a toad or cat, but sometimes with all at once. He speaks with a hoarse voice.

THE SEAL OF BAAL

II. AGARES, a duke ruling in the East, who appears in the form of a comely old man, ambling upon a crocodile and carrying a goshawk on his wrist. He makes those who run stand still, brings back runaways, teaches all languages, destroys spiritual and temporal dignities, and causes earthquakes. He is of the Order of the Virtues.

III. VASSAGO, a mighty prince, of the nature of Agares, who declares things past, present, and future, and discovers what has been lost or hidden. He is good by nature.

THE SEAL OF AGARES

THE SEAL OF VASSAGO

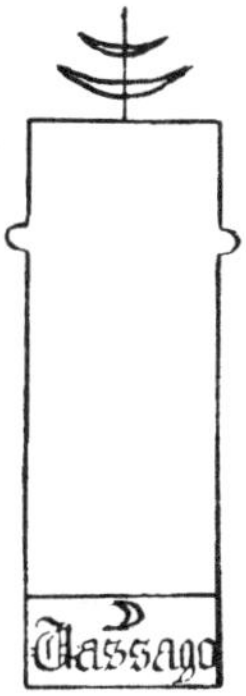

SEAL OF VASSAGO
USED IN WHITE MAGIC

IV. GAMYGYN, a great marquis, appearing in the form of a small horse or ass, but afterwards in human shape. He speaks hoarsely, teaching the liberal sciences, and giving news of souls who have died in sin.

V. MARBAS, a president, who appears as a mighty lion, and then in human shape. He answers truly concerning all things hidden or secret, causes and cures diseases, imparts skill in mechanics, and changes men into various shapes. VI. Valefor, a powerful duke, appearing as a many headed lion. He leads those with whom he is familiar into theft.

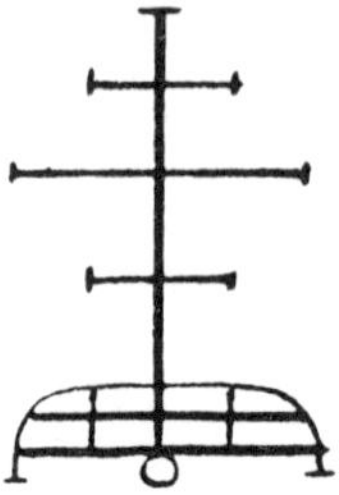

THE SEAL OF GAMYGYN

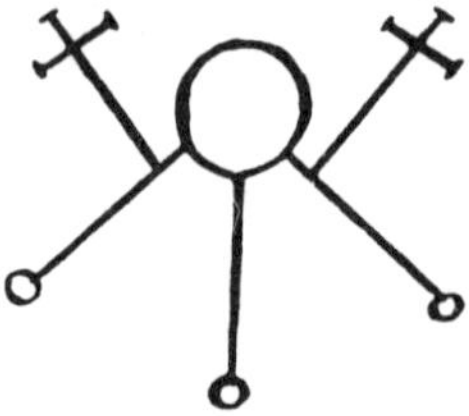

THE SEAL OF MARBAS

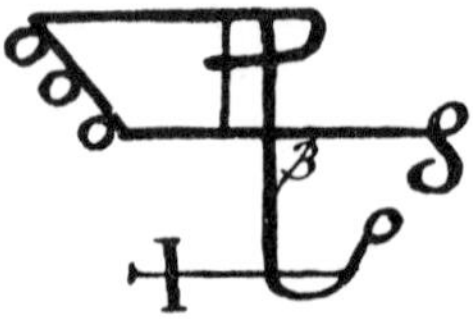

THE SEAL OF VALEFOR

VII. Amon, a strong and powerful marquis, who appears like a wolf with a serpent's head, and vomiting flame. When so ordered, he assumes a human shape, but with the teeth of a dog. He discerns past and future, procures love, and reconciles friends and foes.

THE SEAL OF AMON

VIII. Barbatos, a great count and duke, who appears when the sun is in Sagittarius with four noble kings and three companies of troops; he gives instruction in all the sciences, reveals treasures concealed by enchantment, knows the past and future, reconciles friends and those in power, and is of the Order of the Virtues.

THE SEAL OF BARBATOS

IX. Paimon, a great king, very obedient to Lucifer. He appears like a crowned man seated on a dromedary, preceded by all manner of musicians. He speaks with a roaring voice, teaches all arts, sciences, and secrets, gives and confirms dignities, makes men subject to the will of the Magician, provides good familiars. He is observed towards the north-west, and is of the Order of Dominions.

THE SEAL OF PAIMON

X. BUER, a great president, who appears when the sun is in Sagittarius, and teaches philosophy, logic, the virtues of herbs, &c. He heals all diseases and gives good familiars.
XI. GUSION, a mighty duke, who appears like a cynocephalus, and discerns the past, present, and future, answers all questions, reconciles enemies, and gives honour and dignities.

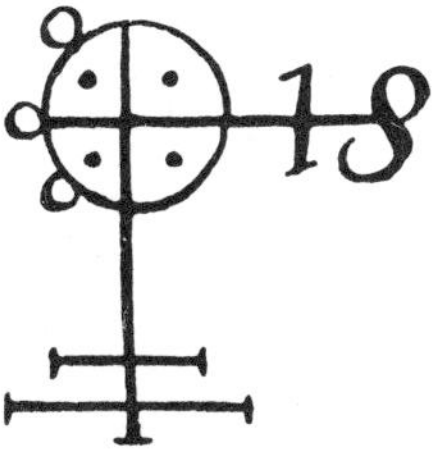

THE SEAL OF BEUR

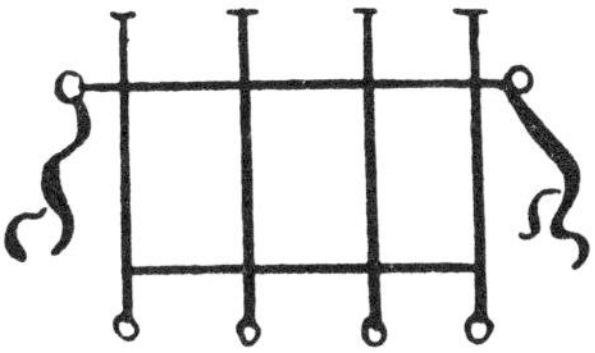

THE SEAL OF GUSION

XII. SYTRY, a great prince, who appears with a leopard's head, but assumes a human form at the Magician's command. He procures love between the two sexes, and causes women to show themselves naked.
XIII. BELETH, a terrible and mighty king, riding on a pale horse, preceded by all manner of musicians. He is very furious when first summoned, and must be commanded into a triangle or circle with the hazel wand of the Magician pointed to the south-east. He must be received courteously and with homage, but a silver ring must be worn on the middle finger of the left hand, which must be held against

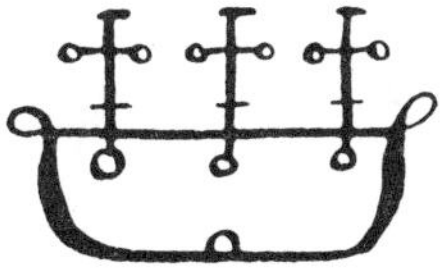

THE SEAL OF SYTRY

THE SEAL OF BELETH

the face. He procures love between man and woman, and is of the Order of the Powers.

XIV. Lerajie, a powerful marquis, coming in the likeness of an archer, clad in green, and bearing bow and quiver. He occasions battles and causes arrow-wounds to putrefy.

XV. Eligor, a great duke, appearing as a goodly knight carrying a lance, pennon, and sceptre. He discovers hidden things, causes war, marshals armies, kindles love and lust.

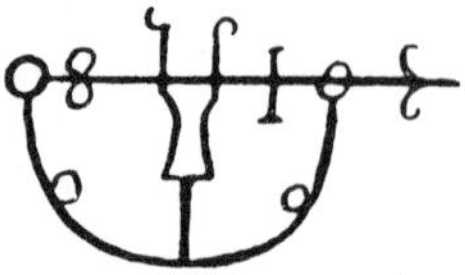

THE SEAL OF LERAJIE

THE SEAL OF ELIGOR

XVI. Zepar, a great duke, who appears in red apparel and armed like a soldier. He inflames women with love for men, and can transform them into other shapes till they have been enjoyed by their lovers.

XVII. Botis, a great president and earl, who appears like a horrid viper, but, when commanded, assumes a human shape, with large teeth and horns. He bears a sharp sword in his hand, discerns past, present, and future, and reconciles friends and foes.

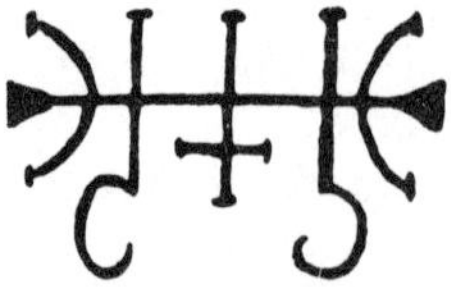

THE SEAL OF ZEPAR

THE SEAL OF BOTIS

XVIII. Bathin, a mighty duke, who appears like a strong man with a serpent's tail, riding on a pale horse. He knows the virtues of herbs and precious stones, and can transport men swiftly from one country to another.

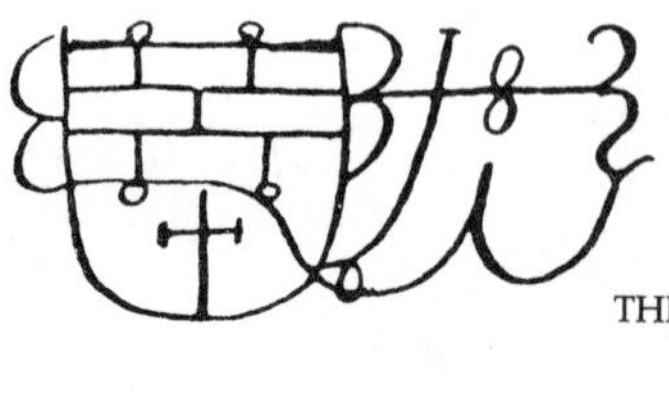

THE SEAL OF BATHIN

XIX. SALEOS, a great duke, who appears like a brave soldier, riding on a crocodile crowned. He promotes love between the sexes.

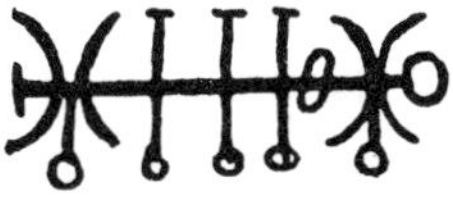

THE SEAL OF SALEOS

XX. PURSON, a great king, who appears like a lion-headed man, carrying a viper in his hand, and riding on a bear, preceded by many trumpeters. He conceals and discovers treasure, discerns past, present, and future, gives true answers concerning things human and divine, and provides good familiars.

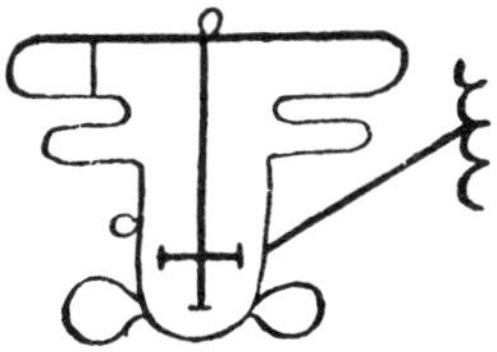

THE SEAL OF PURSON

XXI. MORAX, a great earl and president, who appears like a human-headed bull, and gives skill in astronomy and the liberal sciences, with good familiars. He knows the virtues of all herbs and precious stones.

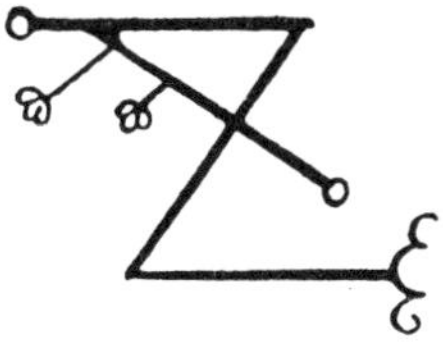

THE SEAL OF MORAX

XXII. IPOS, a mighty earl and prince, appearing as an angel with a lion's head, the webbed feet of a goose, and a hare's

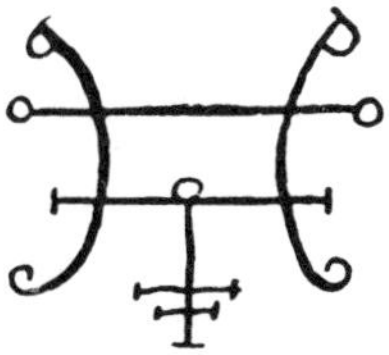

THE SEAL OF IPOS

tail. He knows the past and future, and imparts wit and courage.

XXIII. Aini, a strong duke, who appears with the body of a handsome man and three heads, the first like a serpent, the second like a man with two stars on the forehead, and the third like a cat. He rides on a viper, and carries a blazing firebrand, with which he spreads destruction. He imparts much cunning, and gives true answers concerning private matters.

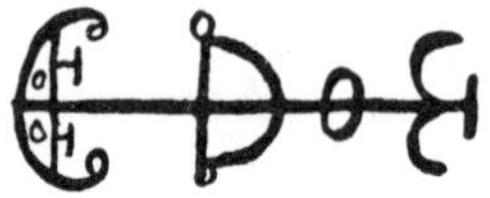

THE SEAL OF AINI

XXIV. Naberius, a valiant marquis, who appears in the form of a crowing cock and flutters about the circle. He speaks hoarsely, gives skill in arts and sciences, especially rhetoric, and restores lost dignities and honours.

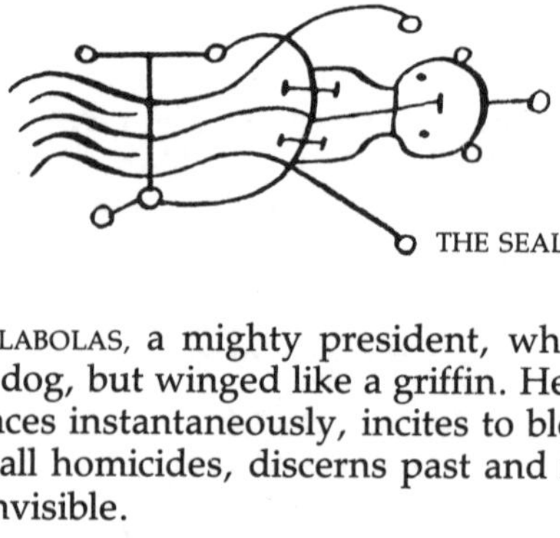

THE SEAL OF NABERIUS

XXV. Glasyalabolas, a mighty president, who comes in the form of a dog, but winged like a griffin. He teaches all arts and sciences instantaneously, incites to bloodshed, is the leader of all homicides, discerns past and future, and makes men invisible.

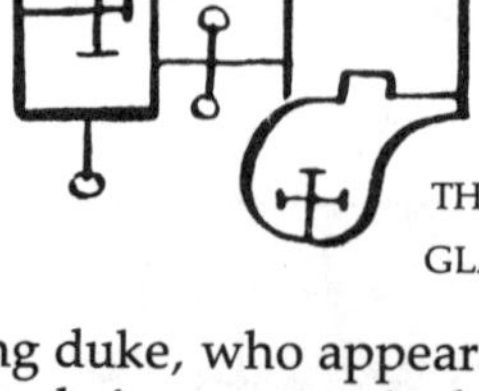

THE SEAL OF GLASYALABOLAS

XXVI. Bune, a strong duke, who appears as a three-headed dragon, the heads being respectively those of a dog, griffin, and man. He has a pleasant voice; he changes the places of the dead, causes demons to crowd round sepulchres, gives riches, makes men wise and eloquent, answers questions truly.

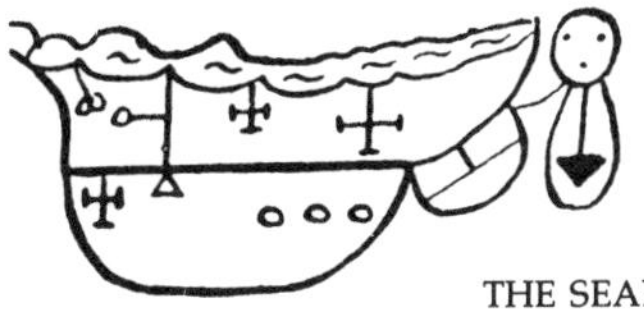

THE SEAL OF BUNE

XXVII. RONOBE, a great marquis and earl, appears in a monstrous form; he teaches rhetoric and the arts, gives a good understanding, the knowledge of tongues, and favour of friends and foes.

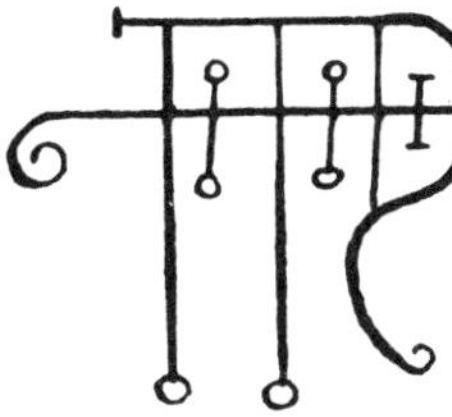

THE SEAL OF RONOBE

XXVIII. BERITH, a terrible duke, appearing in the form of a soldier in red apparel, with a golden crown, and bestriding a red horse. The ring used for Berith is required for his evocation. He gives true answers of things past, present, and to come, turns all metals into gold, gives and confirms dignities. He speaks in a clear and persuasive voice, but is a great liar, and his advice must not be trusted.

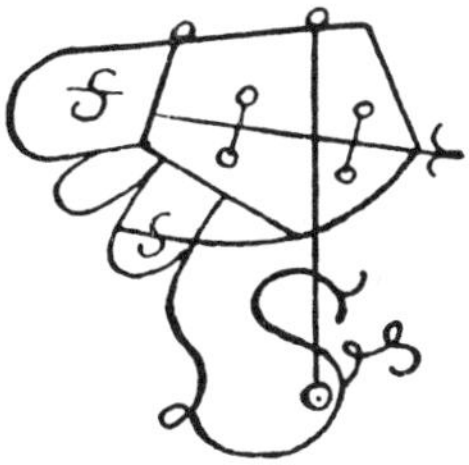

THE SEAL OF BERITH

XXIX. ASTAROTH, a great and powerful duke, appears like a beautiful angel riding on an infernal dragon, and carrying a viper in his right hand. He must not be permitted to approach on account of his stinking breath, and the magician must defend his face with the magic ring. Astaroth answers truly concerning past, present, and future, discovers all secrets, and gives great skill in the liberal sciences. He will also discourse willingly concerning the fall of spirits.

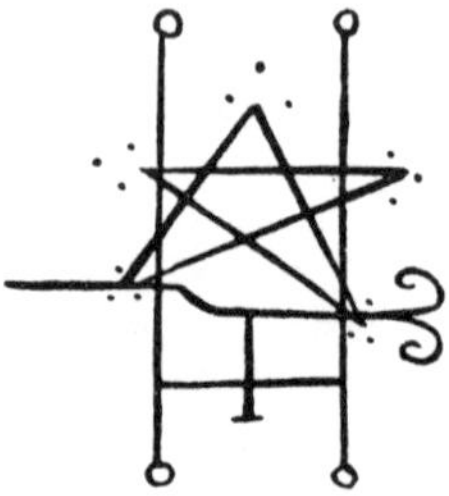

THE SEAL OF ASTAROTH

XXX. Forneus, a great marquis, appears as a sea-monster. He teaches all arts and sciences, gives a good reputation and the knowledge of tongues, and causes men to be loved by their enemies even as by their friends.

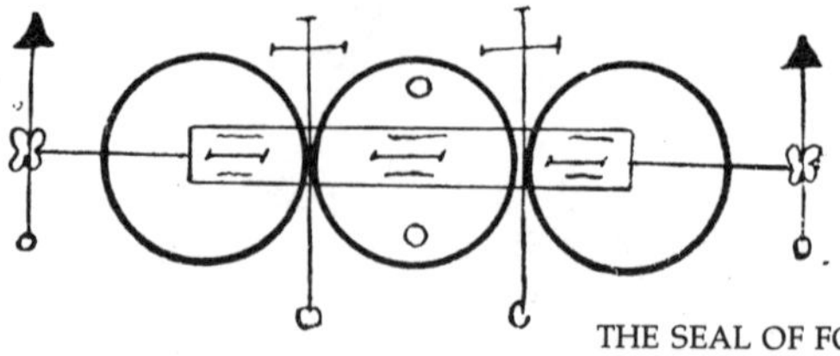

THE SEAL OF FORNEUS

XXXI. Foras, a great president, who appears in the form of a strong man, and teaches the virtues of all herbs and precious stones, as well as logic and ethics; he makes men invisible, imparts wit, wisdom, and eloquence, discovers treasures, and restores things lost.

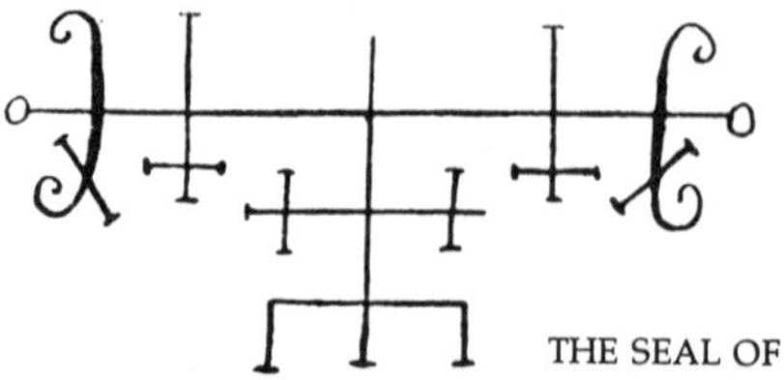

THE SEAL OF FORAS

XXXII. Asmoday, a strong and powerful king, appears with three heads, the first like a bull, the second like a man, and the third like a ram. He has a serpent's tail, the webbed feet of a goose, and he vomits fire. He rides an infernal dragon, carries lance and pennon, and is the chief of the power of Amaymon. He must be invoked bareheaded, for otherwise he will deceive. He gives the ring of virtues, teaches arithmetic, geomancy, and all handicrafts, answers all questions, makes men invisible, indicates the places of concealed treasures, and guards them if within the dominion of Amaymon.

THE SEAL OF ASMODAY

XXXIII. Gaap, a great president and prince, appears when the sun is in the southern signs, coming in a human shape, and preceded by four powerful kings. He teaches philosophy and the liberal sciences, excites love and hatred, makes men insensible, gives instruction in the consecration of those things which belong to the divination of Amaymon, his king, delivers familiars out of the custody of other Magicians, gives true answers as to past, present, and future, transports and returns men speedily from place to place at the will of the exorcist.

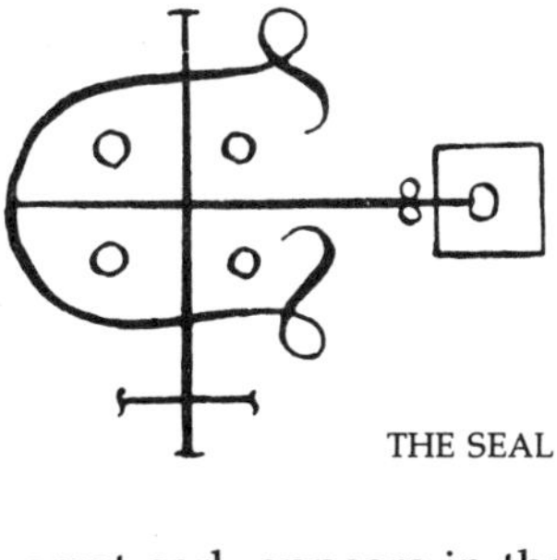

THE SEAL OF GAAP

XXXIV. Furfur, a great earl, appears in the form of a hart with a fiery tail, and will not speak till compelled within the triangle. He then assumes the form of an angel, speaking with a hoarse voice. He causes love between man and wife, raises thunder, lighting, and great winds, gives true answers about secret and divine things.

THE SEAL OF FURFUR

XXXV. Marchosias, a mighty marquis, appears in the form of a wolf with the wings of a griffin, a serpent's tail, and fire issuing from his mouth. At the command of the operator he assumes a human form. He is strong in battle, gives true answers to all questions, and is extremely faithful to the exorcist. He belongs to the Order of Dominations.

THE SEAL OF MARCHOSIAS

XXXVI. Solas or stolas, a powerful prince, appears in the likeness of a raven and then as a man. He teaches the art of astronomy and the virtues of herbs and stones.

XXXVII. Phœnix, a great marquis, appears like the bird of that name, singing dulcet notes in a child's voice. When he assumes human shape at the will of the Magician, he speaks marvellously of all sciences, proves an excellent poet, and fulfils orders admirably. He hopes to return to the Seventh Thrones in 1200 years.

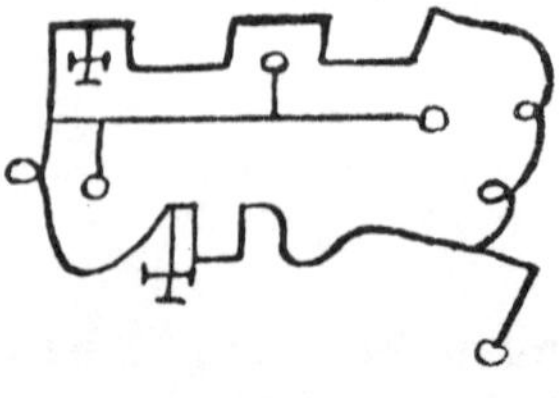

THE SEAL OF SOLAS

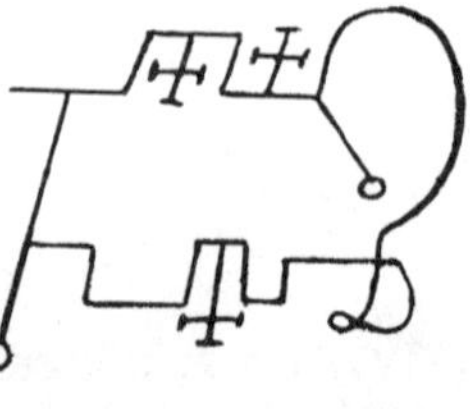

THE SEAL OF PHŒNIX

XXXVIII. HALPAS, a great earl, appears in the form of a stockdove, speaking with a hoarse voice. He burns towns, visits the wicked with the sword, and can send men to fields of war or to other places.
XXXIX. MALPAS, a powerful president, appears at first like a crow, but afterwards, when so commanded, assumes a human form, speaking with a hoarse voice. He brings artificers swiftly from all parts of the world, destroys the desires and thoughts of enemies, gives good familiars, and receives a sacrifice kindly, but will deceive him who offers it.

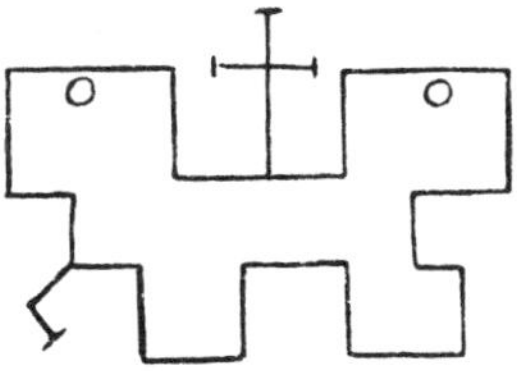

THE SEAL OF HALPAS

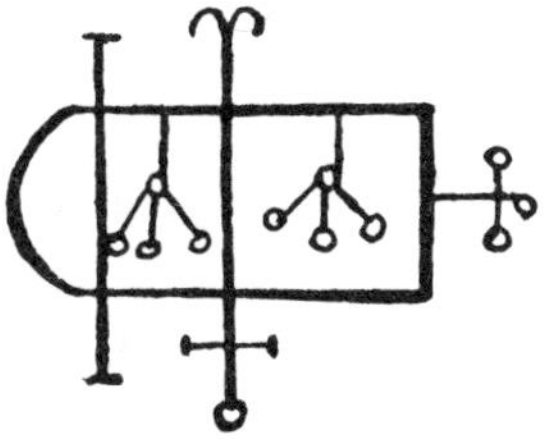

THE SEAL OF MALPAS

XL. RAUM, a great earl, appears in the form of a crow, but assumes human shape when bidden. He steals treasure and carries it where commanded; he destroys cities and dignities; he discerns past, present, and future; he causes love between friends and foes. Finally, he is of the Order of the Thrones.

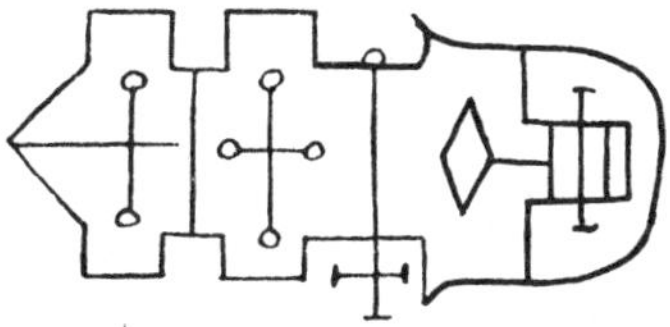

THE SEAL OF RAUM

XLI. FOCALOR, a strong duke, appears in the form of a man with the wings of a griffin. He drowns men, sinks warships, and has power over the winds and the sea, but he will not hurt any one if commanded to forbear by the exorcist. He hopes to return to the Seventh Thrones in 1050 years.
XLII. SABNACK, a mighty marquis, appears in the form of an

armed soldier, having a lion's head, and riding on a pale-coloured horse. He builds towers, camps, and cities, fortifies the same, torments men with wounds and putrid sores swarming with worms; he gives good familiars.

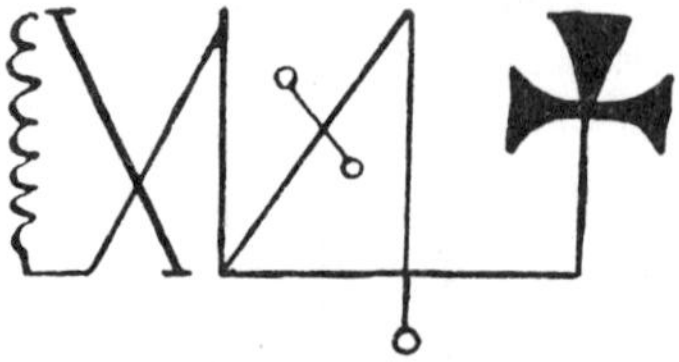

THE SEAL OF FOCALOR

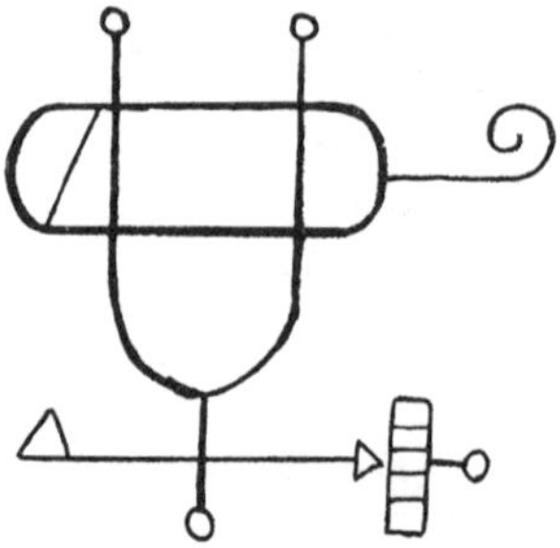

THE SEAL OF SABNACK

XLIII. VEPAR, a great duke, appears as a mermaid. He guides the waters and battleships, and occasions storms at sea when so commanded by the Magician. He also causes the sea to seem full of ships, and occasions death in three days by means of putrefying sores and worm-eaten wounds.

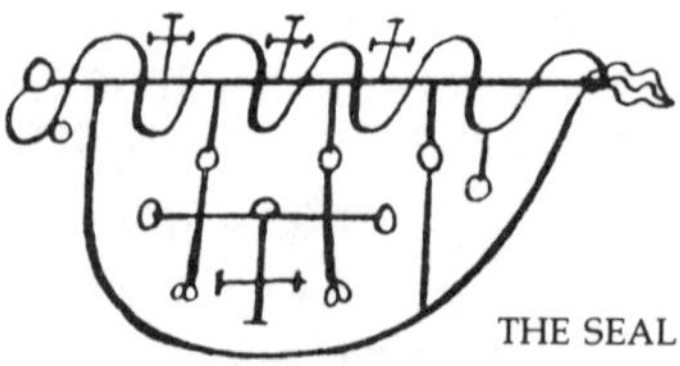

THE SEAL OF VEPAR

XLIV. SHAX, a great marquis, comes in the form of a stockdove, speaking with a hoarse voice. He destroys the sight, hearing, and understanding of any man or woman at the will of the exorcist, steals money from the king's exchequer, and returns it in 1200 years. He will transport anything, but must first be commanded into the triangle; otherwise he will deceive the operator. He discovers all hidden things which are not in the keeping of wicked spirits, and gives good familiars.

XLV. VINE, a great king and earl, appears in a monstrous form, but assumes human shape when commanded, He discerns things hidden, reveals witches, and makes known the past, present, and future. At the command of the exorcist he will build towers, demolish walls, and make the waters stormy.

THE SEAL OF SHAX

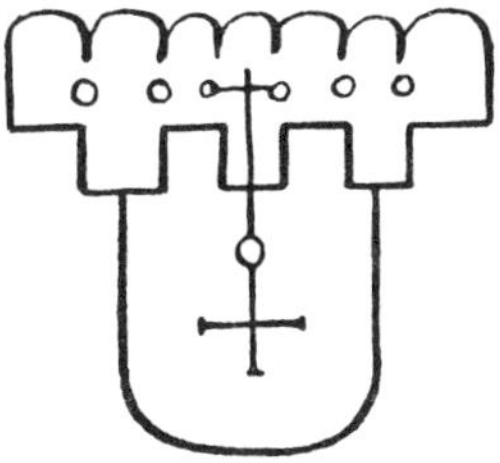

THE SEAL OF VINE

XLVI. Bifrons, a great earl, appears in a monstrous form, but assumes the human shape when commanded. He gives proficiency in astrology, geometry, and other mathematical arts; he teaches the virtues of herbs, precious stones, and woods; he changes dead bodies, puts them in other places, and lights phantom candles on their graves.

THE SEAL OF BIFRONS

XLVII. Vual, a great duke, comes at first as an enormous dromedary, but afterwards assumes human form and speaks in the Egyptian tongue. He procures the love of women, discerns past, present, and future, and excites friendship even between foes. He was of the Order of the Powers.

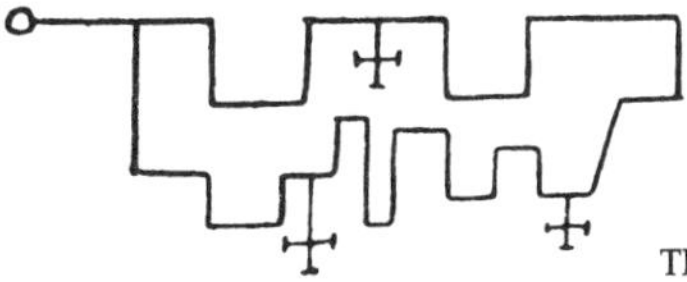

THE SEAL OF VUAL

XLVIII. Hagenti, a great president, appears in the shape of a gigantic bull with the wings of a griffin, but will duly put on human form. He gives wisdom, transmutes all metals into gold, and turns wine into water.

XLIX. Procel appears in the form of an angel, and is a great and strong duke. He speaks mystically of hidden things, teaches geometry and the liberal sciences, and at the command of the operator will make a great commotion like that of running waters; he also warms waters and tempers baths. He was of the Order of the Powers before his fall.

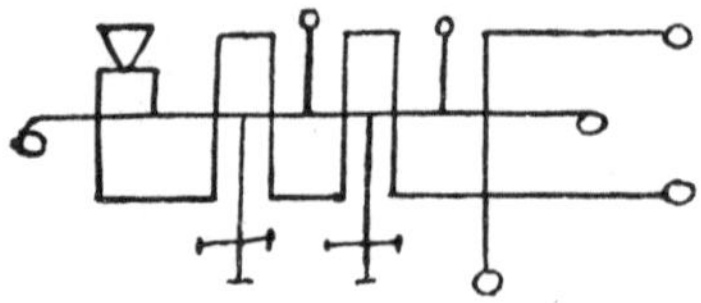

THE SEAL OF HAGENTI

THE SEAL OF PROCEL

L. FURCAS, a great duke, appears in the form of a cruel old man, with long beard and hoary hair. He is seated on a pale horse, and has a sharp spear in his hand. He teaches philosophy, rhetoric, astronomy, logic, chiromancy, and pyromancy, perfectly in all their parts.

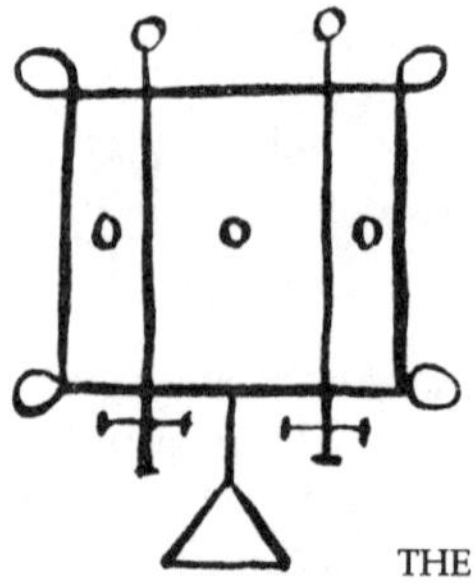

THE SEAL OF FURCAS

LI. BALAM, a terrible and powerful king, appears with three heads, the first like that of a bull, the second like that of a man, and the third like a ram's. With the tail of a serpent and eyes flaming fire, he rides upon a furious bear, carrying a goshawk on his wrist, and speaking with a hoarse voice. He gives true answers as to past, present, and future, makes men go invisible and imparts wit.

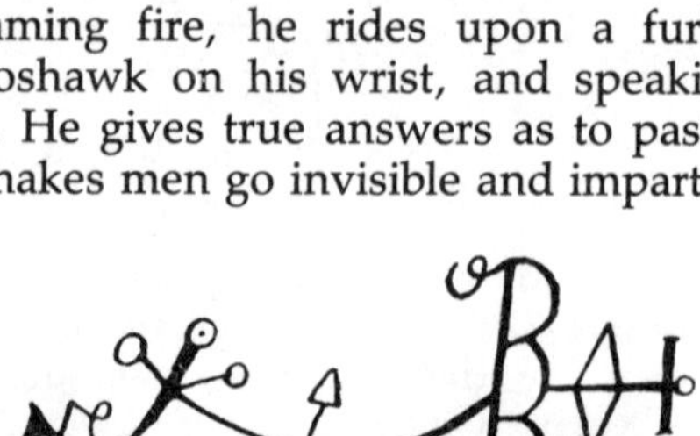

THE SEAL OF BALAM

LII. ALLOCEN, a strong duke, appears in the form of a soldier, mounted on a great horse, his face like that of a lion, exceedingly red, his eyes flaming fire, his speech hoarse and loud. He teaches astronomy and the liberal sciences, and gives a good familiar.

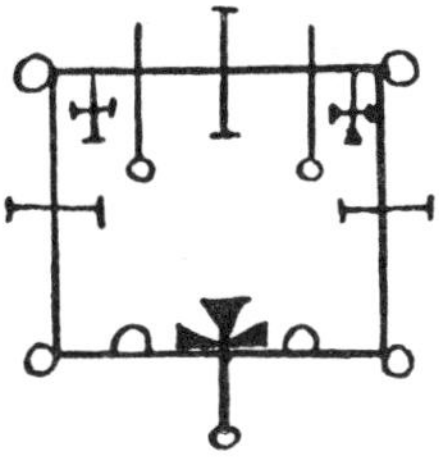

THE SEAL OF ALLOCEN

LIII. CAIM, a great president, appears in the form of a thrush, but afterwards in that of a man bearing a sharp sword, and seeming to answer in burning ashes. He is a keen disputant; he imparts to men the understanding of birds' songs, the lowing of cattle, the barking of dogs, and the voice of waters. He gives true answers concerning things to come, and was once of the Order of Angels.

THE SEAL OF CAIM

LIV. MURMUR, a great duke and earl, appears in the form of a soldier riding on a griffin, and having a duke's crown on his head. He is preceded by two ministers sounding trumpets. He teaches philosophy perfectly, and constrains the souls of the dead to appear and to answer questions. He was partly of the Order of Thrones and partly of Angels.

LV. ORABAS, a great prince, appears first like a horse, but when commanded, in human form. He discovers past, present, and future; he gives good dignities and advancements, with the favour of friends and foes; he will reply concerning the creation of the world and Divinity; he is very faithful to the exorcist, and defends him from temptation by any spirit.

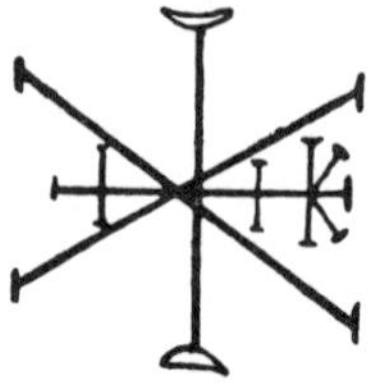

THE SEAL OF MURMUR

THE SEAL OF OROBAS

LVI. GOMORY, a powerful duke, appears like a beautiful woman, wearing a ducal crown. He discovers past, present, and future, as also the whereabouts of hidden treasures; he procures the love of women, and especially of girls.

LVII. OSE, a great president, appears at first like a leopard, and then in human shape. He gives skill in all liberal sciences, and true answers concerning divine and secret things. He can change men into any shape that the exorcist may desire, and he that is changed will not know it.

THE SEAL OF GOMORY

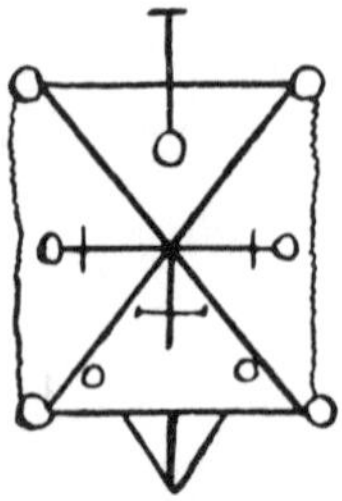

THE SEAL OF OSE

LVIII. AMY, a great president, comes first as a great flaming fire and then as a man. He gives perfect knowledge of astrology and the liberal sciences, with good familiars, and can betray treasures that are kept by spirits.

LIX. ORIAS, a great marquis, appears in the form of a lion bestriding a strong horse; he has a serpent's tail, and holds two enormous hissing snakes in his right hand. He teaches the virtues of the planets and the mansions thereof; he transforms men, gives dignities, prelates, and confirmations, with the favour of friends and foes.

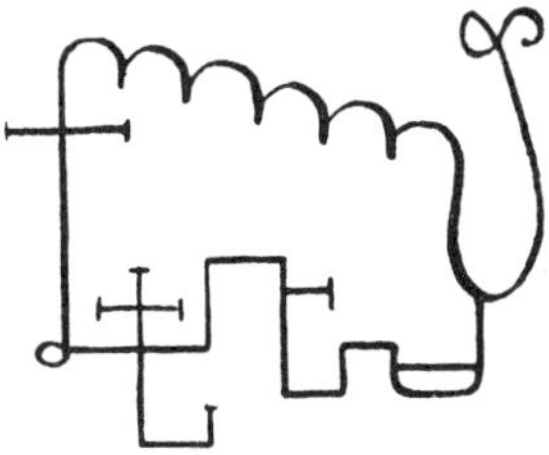

THE SEAL OF AMY

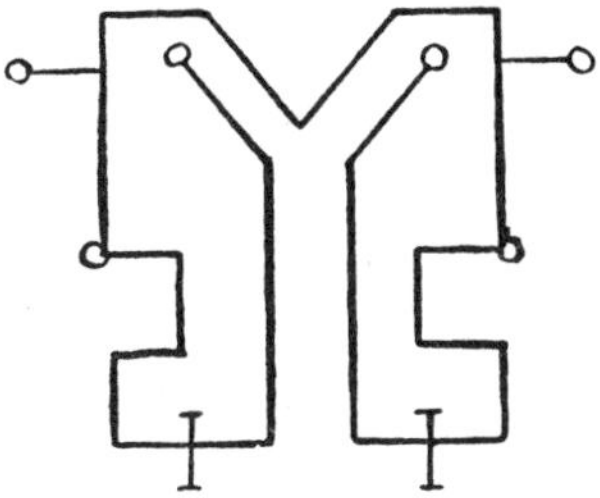

THE SEAL OF ORIAS

LX. VAPULA, a strong duke, comes in the form of a lion with griffin's wings. He gives skill not only in manual professions but also in philosophy and the sciences.

THE SEAL OF VAPULA

LXI. ZAGAN, a great king and president, appears at first in the form of a bull with the wings of a griffin, and after in human shape. He makes men witty, turns water into wine, blood into oil, and oil into water; he can change any metal into coin of the realm, and can make fools wise.

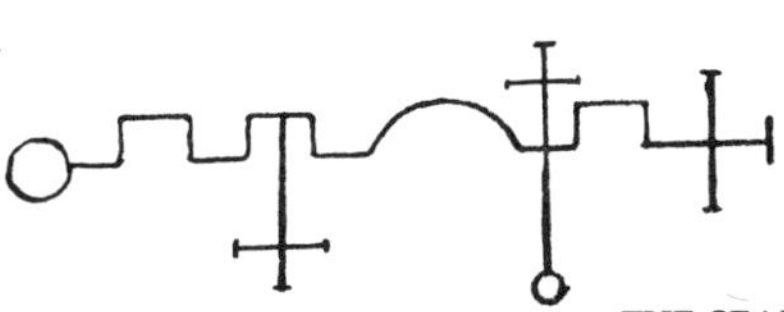

THE SEAL OF ZAGAN

LXII. VALAC, a great president, comes as a little boy with the wings of an angel and riding on a two-headed dragon. He gives true answers concerning hidden treasures, tells where serpents may be seen, and will deliver them helpless to the exorcist.

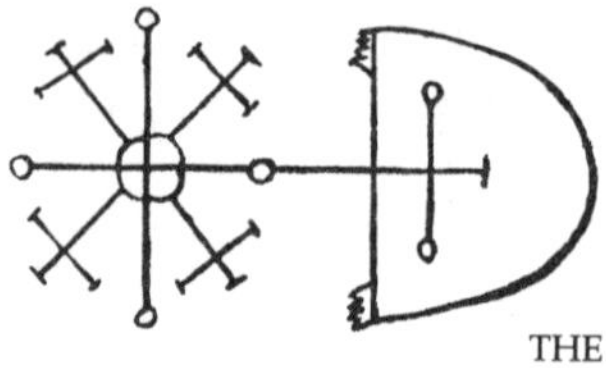

THE SEAL OF VALAC

LXIII. ANDRAS, a great marquis, comes in the form of an angel, with the head of a black night-raven, riding upon a strong black wolf, and having a sharp bright sword gleaming in his hands. He sows discord, and will kill the unwary.

LXIV. FLAUROS, a great duke, appears at first like a terrible leopard, but at the command of the exorcist he puts on the shape of a man, with fiery eyes and terrible countenance. He gives true answers of things past, present, and future, but unless commanded into the triangle he will deceive the exorcist. He converses gladly of divinity and the creation of the world, as also of the fall of spirits, his own included. If desired, he will destroy and burn the enemies of the operator, nor will he suffer him to be tempted by spirits or otherwise.

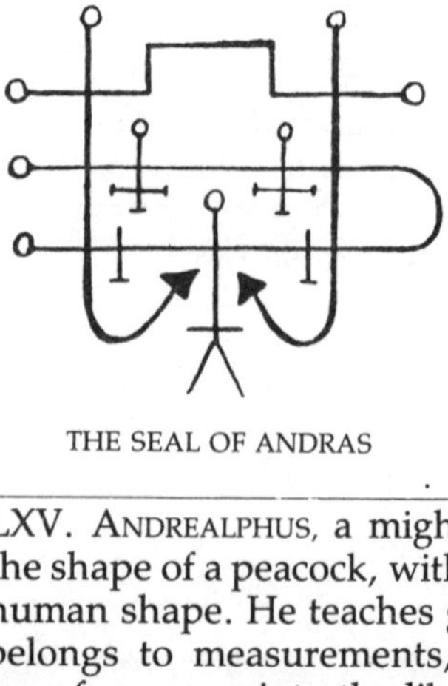

THE SEAL OF ANDRAS

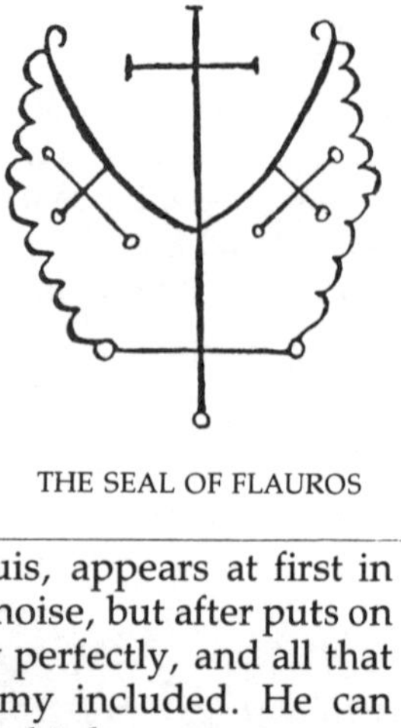

THE SEAL OF FLAUROS

LXV. ANDREALPHUS, a mighty marquis, appears at first in the shape of a peacock, with a great noise, but after puts on human shape. He teaches geometry perfectly, and all that belongs to measurements, astronomy included. He can transform men into the likeness of a bird.

LXVI. CIMERIES, a powerful marquis, appears like a valiant

soldier on a black horse. He rules the spirits in the parts of Africa; he teaches grammar, logic, and rhetoric, discovers hidden treasures and things lost and hidden; he can make a man appear like a soldier of his own kind.

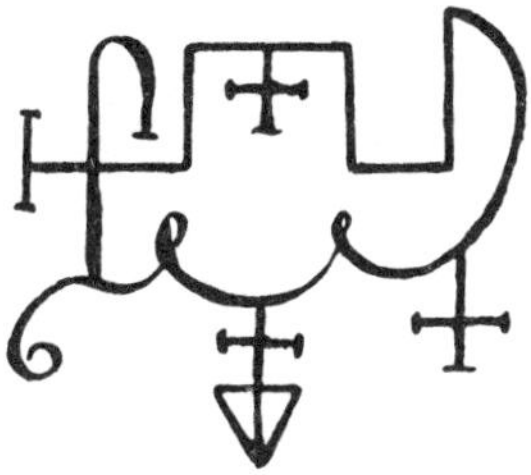

THE SEAL OF ANDREALPHUS

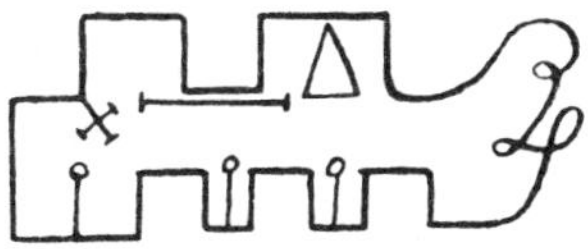

THE SEAL OF CIMERIES

LXVII. AMDUSCIAS, a great duke, comes first like a unicorn, but will stand up at request in human shape, causing all manner of musical instruments to be heard but not seen. He makes trees fall at the will of the operator, and gives excellent familiars.

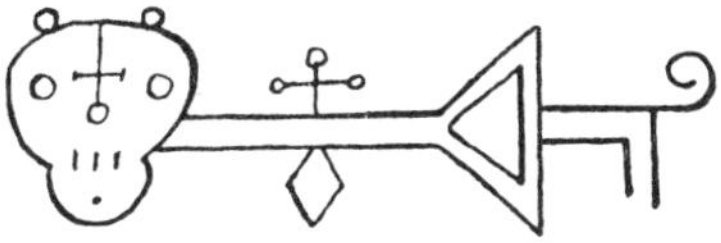

THE SEAL OF AMDUSCIAS

LXVIII. BELIAL, a mighty king, created next after Lucifer, appears in the form of a beautiful angel seated in a chariot of fire, and speaking with a pleasant voice. He fell first amongst the superior angels who went before Michael and other heavenly angels. He distributes preferences of senatorships, causes favours of friends and foes, and gives excellent familiars. He must have offerings and sacrifices made to him.

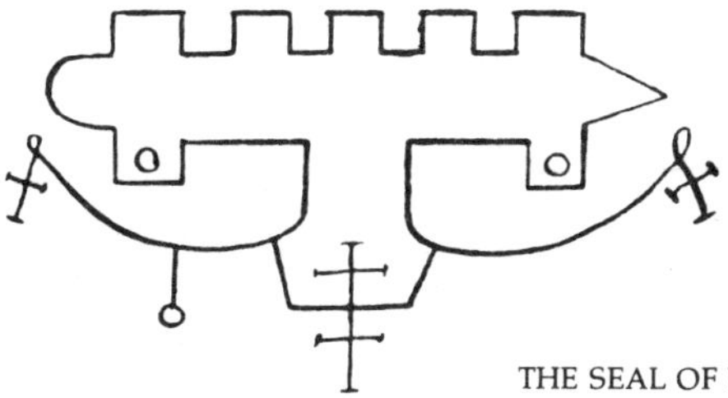

THE SEAL OF BELIAL

LXIX. Decarabia, a marquis, comes in the form of a star in a pentacle, but puts on the image of man at command. He discovers the virtues of herbs and precious stones, makes birds seem to fly before the exorcist, and remain with him as familiars, singing and eating like other birds.

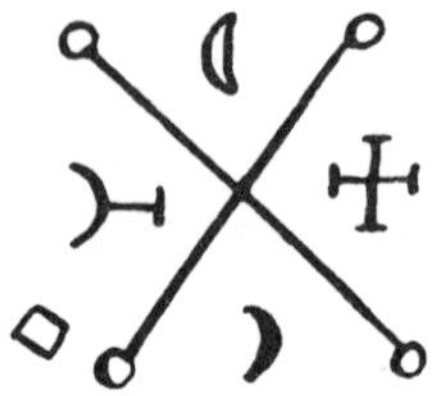

THE SEAL OF DECARABIA

LXX. Seere, a mighty prince under Amaymon, King of the East, appearing in the form of a beautiful man on a strong winged horse. He brings all things to pass suddenly, transports to any place in the twinkling of an eye, and discovers all thefts. He is indifferently good or bad, and will do the will of the operator.

THE SEAL OF SEERE

LXXI. Dantalian, a mighty duke, appears in the form of a man with many faces of men and women, and has a book in his right hand. He teaches all arts and sciences, declares all secret counsels, for he knows all human thoughts, and can change them at his will. He kindles love, and shows the similitude of any person in a vision, wheresoever they may be.

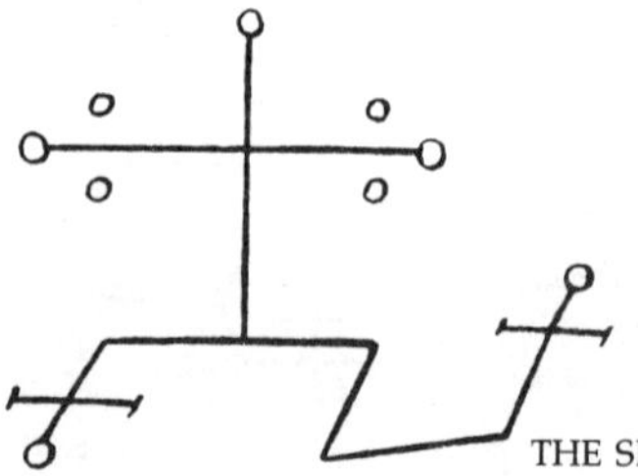

THE SEAL OF DANTALIAN

LXXII. ANDROMALIUS, a great duke and earl, appears in the form of a man holding a serpent in his hand. He returns stolen goods and the thief, discovers all wickedness and underhand dealing, as also hidden treasures.

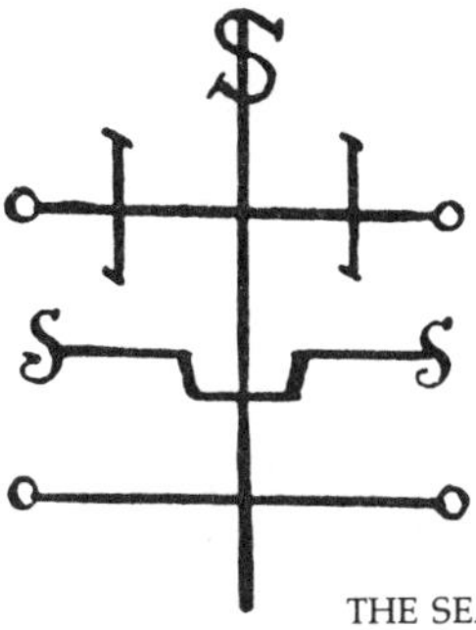

THE SEAL OF ANDROMALIUS

22.
The Pauline Art of Solomon

The following extracts are from a manuscript copied out by Frederick Hockley, the indefatigable nineteenth-century collector of occult documents. I am indebted to its owner, R.A. Gilbert, for drawing my attention to it and allowing me to quote from it. Hockley's preface to this grimoire states: 'The MS from which this copy is transcribed is dated 1715 and is very finely written in red and black with coloured seals. It appears to be a copy of a MS bearing the date 1641, but the original work itself is of a very remote date being mentioned by Agrippa in his Occult Philosophy, 4to 1533, and Scott in his work on Witchcraft, 4to 1584, Gaffarel, Trithemius etc. etc.'

The text of the *Pauline Art* contains the kind of information encountered in many other grimoires: names of angels and demons, their seals, the hours of the day that they rule and how to conjure and invoke them. Here is the conjuration of Samael:

> Thou mighty, great and potent prince Samael who ruleth in the first hour of the day, I the servant of the most high God do conjure and entreat thee a servant of the most Omnipotent and Immortal Lord God of Hosts Jehovah Tetragrammaton and by the name and in the name of that God you owe obedience to and by the hierarchy and by the seal and mark you are known in power by, and by the seven angels who stand before the throne of God and by the seven planets and by their seals and characters and by the angel that ruleth the sign of the 12th house now ascending in the first hour, that thou will graciously be pleased to gird up and gather thyself

> together and by divine permission to move and come from all parts of the world wheresoever you be and show thyself visibly and plainly in this chrystal stone to the sight of my eyes speaking with a voice intelligible and to my understanding and that you would be so favorably pleased that I may have thy familiar friendship and constant society both now and at all other times when I shall call thee forth to visible appearance and to inform and direct me in all things that shall seem good to the great Creator and thee.
>
> O thou great and powerful Angel Samael I invocate, adjure, command and most powerfully call you forth from your order and place of residence to visible appearance by the great God who was and is and ever shall be …

After this formula of conjuration, there follows a formula of invocation in which the magician begins by invoking the chief angel of the appropriate hour of the day, before proceeding to summon any of the subsidiary angels. Here the magician calls upon the chief angel of the hour 'to send me and cause to come and appear unto me all or any of the angels that I shall call by name that are resident under your government'. He goes on to request that these angels 'do in secret help and assist me in all such matters and things according to their office as I shall desire or request …'

One somehow imagines the magician delivering these words in the tone of a rather fussy solicitor, anxious to do everything according to form and not offend the angels by infringing the order of precedence.

NOTES

Chapter 1: The World of the Magician

1. Op. cit., Vol. III (Edinburgh, T. & T. Clark, 1915), p. 245.
2. Op. cit., abridged edition (London, Macmillan, 1963), p. 50.
3. Aleister Crowley, *Magick in Theory and Practice* (Paris, Lecram Press, 1929), p. xvi.
4. Op. cit. (London, C.W. Daniel, undated, *c*. 1976), p. 9.

Chapter 2: The Roots of the Occult Tradition

1. Op. cit. (London, Kegan Paul, Trench, Truebner & Co., undated).
2. Franz Cumont, *The Oriental Religions in Roman Paganism* (Chicago, Open Court Publishing Company, 1911).
3. See also R.H.W. Empson, *The Cult of the Peacock Angel* (London, Witherby, 1928).
4. F.C. Conybeare, 'The Testament of Solomon', *Jewish Quarterly Review*, Vol. XI (London, 1899).
5. For an account of the lower entities, see Mathers on the demons of the Qliphoth in R.A. Gilbert's anthology *The Sorcerer and His Apprentice* (Wellingborough, Aquarian Press, 1983).

Chapter 3: Early Magical Texts

1. Op. cit., Vol. I (Leipzig/Berlin, B.G. Teubner, 1928).
2. Quoted from B.R. Rees, 'Magical Papyri' in *Man, Myth and Magic*, Vol. 60 (London, BPC Publishing, 1971).
3. *The Golden Ass of Lucius Apuleius*, translated by William Adlington, 1566, chapter 17. The spelling has been modernized.

4. Franz Cumont, *The Oriental Religions in Roman Paganism*.
5. Johann Hartlieb, *Buch aller verbotenen Kunst*, quoted in preface to *Picatrix*, translated by Helmut Ritter and Martin Plessner (London, Warburg Institute, 1962).
6. *Picatrix*, translated by Ritter and Plessner.
7. Ibid.
8. Ibid.
9. Ibid.
10. Henry Corbin, *The Man of Light in Iranian Sufism*, translated by Nancy Pearson (Boulder and London, Shambhala, 1978).
11. *Picatrix*, Book II, Chapter 6. Also quoted by Corbin, p. 18.

Chapter 4: All Solomon's Wisdom

1. Gershom Scholem, *The Messianic Idea in Judaism* (London, George Allen and Unwin, 1971), p. 264.
2. Lynn Thorndike, *A History of Magic and Experimental Science*, Vol. II (New York, Macmillan, 1929), pp. 279–280.
3. E.M. Butler, *Ritual Magic* (California, Newcastle Publishing Company, 1971), p. 48.
4. *The Greater Key of Solomon*, translated from ancient manuscripts in the British Museum, London, by S. Liddell MacGregor Mathers, edited by L.W. de Laurence (Chicago, de Laurence Company, 1914).
5. *Encyclopedia of the Unexplained*, edited by Richard Cavendish (London, Routledge and Kegan Paul, 1974), p. 137.
6. *The Greater Key of Solomon*.

Chapter 5: Other Names to Conjure With

1. Lynn Thorndike, *A History of Magic and Experimental Science*, Vol. I, p. 294.
2. Frances A. Yates, *Giordano Bruno and the Hermetic Tradition* (London, Routledge and Kegan Paul, 1964), pp. 44–5.
3. Thorndike, *A History of Magic and Experimental Science*, Vol. I, p. 288.
4. Ibid., p. 343.

5. Thorndike, Vol. II, pp. 284–8.
6. Eliphas Lévi, La clef des grande mystères (Paris, 1897 and London, Rider, 1969).

Chapter 6: Magic and the Church

1. Thorndike, Vol. I, p. 722.
2 Heinrich Reusch, *Index der verbotenen Bücher* (2 vols., Bonn, Verlag von Max Cohen & Sohn, 1883 and 1885).
3. F.W. Lehmberg (editor), *Ceremonial-Magie I: 22 Hauptwerke mittelalterlicher Magie,* Moonchild-Edition 10 (Munich, Arbeitsgemeinschaft für Religions- und Weltanschauungsfragen, 1978).

Chapter 7: Doctor Universalis

1. I have relied on the following two editions of Albertus's work:
(i) *The Book of Secrets of Albertus Magnus, also A Book of the Marvels of the World,* edited by Michael R. Best and Frank H. Brightman (Oxford, Clarendon Press, 1973).
(ii) *Le grand et le petit Albert,* with preface by Bernard Husson (Paris, Editions Pierre Belfond, 1970 and 1978).

Chapter 8: The Strange Case of Nicolas Flamel and the Book of Abraham the Jew

1. Quoted in *The Magical Writings of Thomas Vaughan,* translated and edited by A.E. Waite (London, Redway, 1888), pp. 112–113.

Chapter 9: The Faust Legend

1. Quotations are from Goethe's *Faust,* Part I, translated by Philip Wayne (Penguin Books, 1949).
2. E.M. Butler, *Ritual Magic* (Cambridge University Press, 1949; California, Newcastle Publishing Company, 1971), p. 168.
3. Ibid., p. 198.

Chapter 10: The Golden Age of Magic

1. Frances A. Yates, *Giordano Bruno and the Hermetic Tradition* (London, Routledge and Kegan Paul, 1964), p. 41.
2. Ibid., p. 49.

3. Ibid., p. 53.
4. Ibid., p. 84.
5. *The Steganographia of Johannes Trithemius*, Edited, with an introduction by Adam McLean (Edinburgh, Magnum Opus Hermetic Sourceworks, 1982), p. 1.
6. Ibid., pp. 3–4.
7. Ibid., p. 18.
8. Ibid., p. 22.
9. Ibid., p. 25.
10. *The Hermetic Journal*, No. 19, spring 1983, Editorial, p. 2.
11. This edition was re-issued in 1978 with an introduction by Stephen Skinner (London, Askin Publishers).
12. E.M. Butler, *Ritual Magic*, pp. 155–6.
13. Robert Turner's English translation appeared in 1656 and was reprinted in 1975 with an introduction by Stephen Skinner (London, Askin/New York, Weiser).
14. *The Magical Calendar of Tycho Brahe*, edited by Adam McLean (Edinburgh, Magnum Opus Hermetic Sourceworks, 1979), p. v.

Chapter 11: John Dee and the Enochian Writings

1. Donald C. Laycock, *The Complete Enochian Dictionary* (London, Askin Publishers, 1978). See also Leo Vinci, *Gmicalzoma! An Enochian Dictionary* (London and New York, Regency Press, 1976).
2. Quatercentennial edition of the Magical Writings of John Dee, edited by Adam McLean (Edinburgh, Magnum Opus Hermetic Sourceworks). Vol. I, *De Heptarchia Mystica*, 1983.

Chapter 12: The Sixth and Seventh Books of Moses

1. Will-Erich Peuckert, 'das Sechste und Siebente Buch Mosis', in *Zeitschrift für deutsche Philologie*, Vol. 76, 1957 (Berlin, Erich Schmidt Verlag).
2. MS number 2537 in the Darmstadt State Library. This was copied from an earlier MS in about 1800.
3. Herbert Leventhal, *In the Shadow of the Enlightenment: Occultism and Renaissance Science in Eighteenth-Century America* (Princeton University Press, 1974), pp. 107–9.
4. Kelpius's manuscript was entitled *Phisica, Metaphisica*

et Hyperphisica. D.O.M.A. Manley Palmer Hall was responsible for editing and publishing the manuscript under the title of *Codex Rosae Crucis* (Philosophical Research Society, 1938, second edition, 1971). See also my *Rosy Cross Unveiled* (Aquarian Press, 1980).
5. Leventhal, pp. 107–9.
6. Ibid.
7. *The Sixth and Seventh Books of Moses* (Chicago, de Laurence, 1910).
8. *The Original Key to the Sixth and Seventh Books of Moses* (Bombay, no date or publisher's imprint).

Chapter 13: Magic in the Nineteenth Century
1. See John Hamill, *Frederick Hockley, The Rosicrucian Seer* (Wellingborough, Aquarian Press, 1985).
2. *The Magus*, by Francis Barrett, introduced by Timothy d'Arch Smith (paperback edition, Secaucus, New Jersey, Citadel Press, 1980), pp. iv–v.
3. Ibid., Book I, p. 25.
4. Ibid., Book I, p. 27.
5. Ibid., Book I, pp. 87–88.
6. Ibid., Book II, p. 7.
7. Ibid., Book II, p. 22.
8. Op. cit., 1825 edition, p. ix.
9. Ibid., p. 210.
10. Ibid., pp. 217–18.
11. Ibid., pp. 220–21.
12. Ibid., pp. 232–3.
13. Ibid., p. 240.
14. Ibid., pp. 509–11.
15. Op. cit., chapter 7.
16. Eliphas Lévi, *Transcendental Magic: its Doctrine and Ritual*, translated by A.E. Waite (London, Rider, 1968), p. 296.
17. Ibid., p. 297.

Chapter 14: The Book of Abra-Melin
1. *The Book of the Sacred Magic of Abra-Melin the Mage*, translated by S.L. MacGregor-Mathers (Wellingborough, Thorsons, 1976), pp. xvi–xx.
2. Ibid., p. 56.

3. Ibid., pp. 74–5.
4. Ibid., p. 84.
5. Georges Chevalier, *The Sacred Magician: a Ceremonial Diary* (London, Paladin, 1976), p. 94.

Chapter 15: The Literature of Witchcraft, and Other Modern Grimoires

1. Charles G. Leland, *Aradia, or the Gospel of the Witches of Italy* (London, David Nutt, 1899), Appendix.
2. Ibid., pp. 6–7.
3. Ibid., p. 13.
4. Article by Francis King in the *Encyclopedia of the Unexplained,* edited by Richard Cavendish (London, Routledge and Kegan Paul, 1974), p. 276.
5. *The Grimoire of Lady Sheba* (St Paul, Minnesota, Llewellyn, 1974).

Chapter 16: Grimoires in Literature

1 Evelyn Underhill, *The Column of Dust* (London, Methuen, 1909), Ch. 2.
2. From *The Grimoire and other Supernatural Stories,* collected by Montague Summers (London, Fortune Press, 1936).
3. *H.P. Lovecraft: Selected Letters 1925–1929,* edited by August Derleth and Donald Wandrei (Saule City, Wisconsin, Arkham House, 1968), p. 201.
4. *The Necronomicon,* edited by George Hay, with contributions by Robert Turner, David Langford and Colin Wilson (Jersey, Neville Spearman, 1979, London, Corgi Books, 1980).
5. *The Necronomicon,* edited with an introduction by Simon (New York, Schlangekraft/Barnes Graphics, 1977).

Chapter 17: Talking of the Devil

1. Anton Szandor LaVey, *The Satanic Rituals* (New York, Avon Books, 1972), pp. 16–17.

Chapter 19: Tibetan Magic

1. René de Nebesky-Wojkowitz, *Oracles and Demons of Tibet* (The Hague, Mouton, 1956), Ch. 25.

2. D.L. Snellgrove, *Hevajra Tantra; a Critical Study* (London, Oxford University Press, 1959), Part I, Ch. 2.

BIBLIOGRAPHY

(In most cases the dates given are those of editions most readily available to the author.)

Printed Source Works

Agrippa, Heinrich Cornelius, *De Occulta Philosophia* (Cologne, 1531); published in England as *Three Books of Occult Philosophy* (London, 1651).

(spurious) *Fourth Book of Occult Philosophy*, translated by Robert Turner (London, Askin Publishers, 1978).

Albertus Magnus, *Book of Secrets*, edited by Michael R. Best and Frank H. Brightman (Oxford, Clarendon Press, 1973).

Le Grand et le Petit Albert (Paris, Editions Pierre Belfond, 1978); French version with preface by Bernard Husson, including the probably spurious *Little Albert*.

Ancient Egyptian Magical Texts, translated by J.F. Borghouts (Leiden, E.J. Brill, 1978). collection of spells, mostly from the Middle Kingdom (ie from about 2000 BC).

Babylonion Magic and Sorcery, cuneiform texts translated and introduced by L.W. King (London, Luzac, 1896).

Bardon, Franz, *Initiation into Hermetics* (Koblenz, Osiris-Verlag, 1962).

The Practice of Magical Evocation (Wuppertal, Dieter Rüggeberg, 1975).

Barrett, Francis, *The Magus, or Celestial Intelligencer* (London, 1801). Reprinted, with an introduction by Timothy d'Arch Smith (Secausus, New Jersey, Citadel Press, 1980).

The Book of the Goetia of Solomon the King, edited with a

commentary by Aleister Crowley (Boleskine, 1904).

Buckland, Raymond *The Tree: the Complete Book of Saxon Witchcraft* (York Beach, Maine, Weiser, 1974).

Crowley, Aleister, *Magick in Theory and practice* (1st edn. Paris, 4 vols., privately printed, 1929).

The Devils and Evil Spirits of Babylonia, being Babylonian and Assyrian incantations against the demons, ghouls, vampires, hobgoblins, ghosts, and kindred evil spirits which attack mankind, translated from the original cuneiform texts, with vocabulary and notes by R. Cambell Thompson, 2 vols. (London, Luzac, 1903 and 1904).

Gray, W.G., *Magical Ritual Methods* (Toddington, Helios Books, 1971).

Le Grand Grimoire, ou l'art de commander les esprits célestes (Paris, 1845).

The Grimoire of Armadel, trans. and ed. by S.L. MacGregor Mathers, with introduction and additional notes by Francis King (London, Routledge, 1980).

Le Grimoire du Pape Honorius, many editions including: (a) dated 1800 'à Rome', but probably published in France; (b) dated 1760 'à Rome', but probably issued in France in about 1800, with coloured illustrations and minor textual differences from edition (a); (c) published at Lille in 1840.

Grimorium Verum, editions include: (a) French translation by Plaingière, 1780; (b) French edition dated 1517 'à Memphis, chez Alibeck, l'Egyptien' but probably published in France in about 1817.

The Key of Solomon the King (Clavicula Salomonis), trans. and ed. from ancient manuscripts in the British Museum by S. Liddell Mathers (London, Kegan Paul, Trench, Trübner & Co., 1909), reprinted by Routledge and Kegan Paul, London (latest printing, 1981).

King, Francis, and Skinner, Stephen, *Techniques of High Magic* (London, C.W. Daniel, undated).

The Leiden Magical Papyrus, trans. and presented by Adhémar Massart (Leiden, Brill, 1954).

Lenain, *La Science cabalistique* (Amiens, the author, 1823).

Lévi, Eliphas, *Dogme et rituel de la haute magie* (first published as one volume, Paris, Germer Baillière, 1856). English translation by A.E. Waite (London, Rider, 1968).

Papus (Dr Gérard Encausse), *Traite élémentaire de magie pratique* (Paris, Chacornac, 1906).

Papyri Graecae Magicae, die griechischen Zauberpapyri, herausgegeben und übersetzt von Karl Preisendanz, 2 vols. (Leipzig/Berlin, B.G. Teubner, 1928 and 1931).

Picatrix (Das Ziel des Weisen von Pseudo Magrītī, translated into German from the Arabic by Helmut Ritter and Martin Plessner (London, the Warburg Institute, 1962).

Porta, Giambattista della, *Natural Magic* (English translation, London, 1658, reprinted by Basic Books, New York, 1957).

Regardie, Israel, *The Golden Dawn* (Saint Paul, Minnesota, Llewellyn Publications, 1978).

Scheible, J., *Das Kloster,* 12 vols. (Stuttgart, 1845–49); contains, among other things, valuable source material from the Faustian tradition of magical writing.

Sepher Maphteah Shelomo (Book of the Key of Solomon), an exact facsimile of an original book of magic in Hebrew, introduced by Hermann Gollancz (Oxford University Press, 1914).

Slater, Hermann (ed.), *A Book of Pagan Rituals* (York Beach, Maine, Weiser, 1978).

Snell, Lionel, *SSOTBME, an essay on magic, its foundations, development and place in modern life,* published anonymously (Redbourn, Hertfordshire, The Mouse that Spins, 1975), reprinted 1977.

Thundersqueak, or the Confessions of a Right-Wing Anarchist, published pseudonymously as 'the suicide writings of Liz Angerford and Ambrose Lea'(Luton, The Mouse that Spins, 1979).

These two penetrating works reveal the author to be one of the most important magical thinkers of the twentieth century.

Spare, A.O., *The Collected Works of Austin Osman Spare* (Leeds, The Sorcerer's Apprentice, 1982); contains Spare's *Book of Pleasure,* explaining his system of magical sigils.

Secondary Sources

Butler, E.M., *The Myth of the Magus* (Cambridge University Press, 1948).

Ritual Magic (Cambridge University Press, 1949).
The Fortunes of Faust (Cambridge University Press, 1952).
Three immensely valuable books, particularly in regard to the Faustian tradition.

Deacon, Richard, *John Dee* (London, Muller, 1968).

French, Peter J., *John Dee, the World of an Elizabethan Magus* (London, Routledge and Kegan Paul, 1972).

Gardner, Gerald B., *Witchcraft Today* (London, Rider, 1954).
The Meaning of Witchcraft (London, Aquarian Press, 1959).

Givry, Grillot de, *Witchcraft, Magic and Alchemy,* English translation by J. Courtenay Locke (New York, Dover publications, 1971). Contains a chapter headed 'The Books of the Sorcerers'.

Hartlieb, Johann, *Johann Hartliebs Buch aller verbotenen Kunst,* untersucht und herausgegeben von Dora Ulm (Halle an der Saale, Max Niemayer, 1914), the first publication of Hartlieb's fifteenth-century manuscript.

Reusch, Dr Fr., *Der Index der verbotenen Bücher,* 2 vols. (Benn, Max Cohen & Sohn, 1883 and 1885).

Rhodes, H.T.F., *The Satanic Mass* (London, Rider, 1954).

Seligman, Kurt, *Magic, Supernaturalism and Religion,* published in the United States of America as *The History of Magic* (New York, Pantheon Books, 1948), British edn (London, Allen Lane, the Penguin Press, 1971).

Shah, Idries, *The Secret Lore of Magic: Books of the Sorcerers* (London, Muller, 1957), valuable for its extensive extracts from various grimoires.

Thorndike, Lynn, *A History of Magic and Experimental Science* (New York, Columbia University Press, 1923–58), a formidable, many-volumed work, invaluable for its information on important magical writings of the past.

Waite, A.E., *The Book of Black Magic and of Pacts* (privately printed, 1898), containing extracts from a number of grimoires.

Walker, D.P., *Spiritual and Demonic Magic from Ficino to Campanella* (London, the Warburg Institute, 1958).

Wilson, Colin, *The Occult* (London, Hodder and Stoughton, 1971).

Index